Front cover: Masha Aday, Gete Tebo, and their
children in the Amaro Mountains, Ethiopia.

Back cover: Coffee tree, Wallega, Ethiopia.

Photography credits: All photographs are the work
of Travis Horn, Thornimages.com, except for the
following:

Page 96: Majka Burhardt

Page 94, 95, 97: Peter Doucette

Page 163: Katie Thurmes Gloeckler

Original artwork by Molly Holmberg.
Mollymaps.com

Preceding pages: **Coffee forest in Northern Highlands of Ethiopia.**
Overleaf: **Bubble blowing at Lake Tana.**

CONTENTS

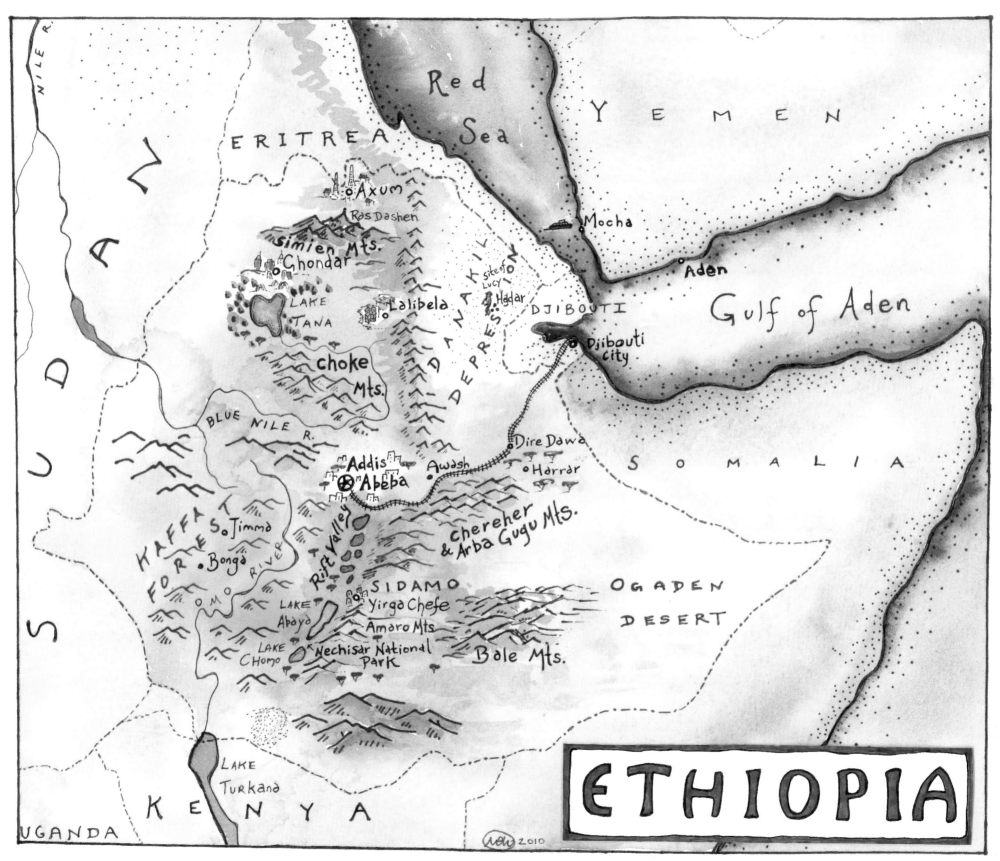

INTRODUCTION

It's a simple question: what if a food crop—coffee—could change a nation's future?

Here are three more questions: What if that crop was something the world had grown to value as a plant starting in the sixth century, and as a brewed infusion in the fifteenth century? What if an assemblage of stories helped shine a collective light on Ethiopia's role as the birthplace of coffee, and its centuries of coffee ritual and culture? And what if sharing these stories deepened the world's understanding of Ethiopia such that perceptions of this nation moved away from struggle and poverty toward strength and bounty?

Our task is Herculean; it will take an optimist. Welcome to *Coffee Story: Ethiopia.* I'm that optimist. I first visited Ethiopia in 2006, as a journalist on a coffee expedition. Like most Americans, my sum-total knowledge of the country consisted of media-fed perceptions of famine, drought, war, poverty, and political strife. As for coffee, all I could tell you was that I liked to drink it. During trips over the next ten years, I grew to know Ethiopia for its lush landscapes, broad lakes, thick forests, towering rock faces, and welcoming people. I came to understand a nation far more complex in its global role and potential than the Western media convey. My initial trip started me on the road to this book. Along the way, I wrote another book about Ethiopia—one that captured its natural beauty through a lens of adventure travel and rock climbing. My and Gabe Rogel's effort, *Vertical Ethiopia: Climbing Toward Possibility in the Horn of Africa,* was the vehicle for my 2008–2009 fifty-city speaking tour across North America. People came to hear tales of Ethiopian exploration, and then stayed for stories about coffee.

During these events, I recognized a need for more information about coffee's role in Ethiopia—not just statistics, but complex stories of real people in a nation with real problems . . . and real potential.

Coffee is the world's most shared connection, chosen daily, with Ethiopia—whether we know it or not. As of 2016, the coffee species indigenous to Ethiopia, Arabica (so named for the Arabs who were the first to cultivate it commercially), comprises 65 percent of the planet's current consumption. Ironically, though all Arabica originally came from Ethiopia, the country's annual coffee production, at 6.5 million sixty-kilogram bags (2016), represents a mere 12 percent of the output of the world's leading producer, Brazil, who in contrast produces 52.1 million bags (77 percent of which is Arabica coffee).

Ethiopia will likely never compete with Brazil in volume, and most cognoscenti would suggest she not even try. But better than volume, Ethiopia holds realms of untapped quality within her borders. This is because, like grapes and wine, coffee has a flavor profile that can differ dramatically between bean varieties. And Ethiopia has more than ten thousand different types of coffee sprouting from her soil. (Colombia, by contrast, has only a handful of primary varieties.)

Specialty coffee, a movement (and term) that started in the 1960s, turned the focus to coffee's quality—a development that spawned a new retailing culture led by Starbucks and similar companies. Today's leading coffee roasters and retailers, along with coffee enthusiasts, place higher value yet on coffees produced via a combination of microclimate, variety, and customized processing. These coffees feed a growing, international, by-the-cup coffee-retailing trend in which the brews are purveyed like fine wines on a list. Ethiopia is the world's second poorest country when ranked by per capita GDP, and twentieth poorest when adjusted for purchasing-power parity (2017), but it has the greatest store of genetic diversity of coffee. Its coffee, if successfully linked with the growing specialty and boutique-specialty coffee trends, can create real results for the country's economy. Ethiopia currently exports 450 million pounds (2016) of coffee per year; a price increase of just $0.10/pound would equal $45 million in additional income.

Whether those who came to my talks were first learning of Ethiopia's role as the birthplace of coffee or knew of it beforehand, they always craved more information about the nation. Coffee created that desire. From the Turkish coffeehouse, to Italian espresso, to the rising appreciation of single-origin specialty coffees, coffee is the most-consumed legal stimulant on Earth. With a growing consumer awareness of food anthropology, coffee drinkers are more

curious than ever about the bean's origins. *Coffee Story: Ethiopia* emerged from that curiosity.

To most of the world, Ethiopia is thought of as barren, flat, and dry. The reality, however, is that two-thirds of Ethiopia is rain-forested highland situated between six hundred and twenty-five hundred meters in altitude, with dark, rich volcanic soil: the perfect place for coffee. It's also the cradle of humanity: the Horn of Africa is more than forty million years old, and fossilized humanoids dating back more than four million years have been found here. No one knows exactly when coffee consumption began. But historians do concur that coffee was integral to Ethiopian life long before the sixth century, when the bean had its first opportunity to be traded over the eighty-kilometer stretch of Red Sea between Ethiopia and Yemen.

In Ethiopia, to drink coffee is to share a story with a friend, family member, or a stranger. Peace is brokered over coffee, religion is celebrated, and in some tribes, coffee can even determine a marriage—for example, in the Amaro Mountains, if a suitor arrives just as a prospective bride's family is drinking a cup from the first of a daily three-round coffee ceremony, the bride must unquestioningly accept his marriage proposal.

But these are only a few snapshots of a nation whose people speak ninety languages and more than two hundred dialects—there is in fact an untold number of stories inside this country of 1.1 million square kilometers. It would take many lifetimes to uncover and share them all.

In the coffee world, we speak of wild coffee thriving in a forest's "understory"—the plants, trees, and shrubs that cover the forest at the ground level, while soaking up protection from the larger trees above. While writing this book, I came to think of the assembled host of tales as coffee's understory.

Coffee Story: Ethiopia is a collection of voices and narratives that reach off the page to stimulate deeper conversation. Rather than a definitive, didactic survey of coffee's cultural uses, *Coffee Story: Ethiopia* is an expressive collage with exploration as its central tenet. The book is assembled as a continuous journey through Ethiopia's most important coffee lands: we start in Kaffa, the genetic home of *Coffee arabica*; journey to Harar, where Ethiopian coffee trade crystallized; travel to the Northern Highlands, home to Tigray, Lake Tana, and the birthplace of the Blue Nile and where ancient coffee practices are still observed; revel in Ethiopia's thriving center—the capital, Addis Ababa—reconnecting with the everyday expression of coffee in this, Africa's third largest city; and finally, adventure in the emerging heartlands of Ethiopian coffee development in the Rift Valley, exploring Sidamo, Yirga Cheffe, and the Amaro Mountains. Other, smaller tales from different regions, as well as essays from coffee-industry insiders, pepper the larger regions. *Coffee Story: Ethiopia* might leave you dizzy. If it does, I have done my job.

Welcome to a conversation about the culture of coffee in the land of coffee's heritage. Welcome to a new vision of Ethiopia . . . .

The first photos in this book—like this one of a Guji family in the Amaro Highlands—were published in Ethiopia, each shot individually with my Polaroid camera as a thank-you for the people who shared their stories with me.

READING NOTES

ETHIOPIA IN SUMMARY

Ethiopia, previously known as Abyssinia, is the only country to have maintained independence against the sixteenth-century Muslim conquest of Ahmad Gragn, the era of European Colonialism, and twentieth-century fascism. This fertile wedge is the "cradle of humanity," where "Lucy," the now-fossilized hominid, lived 3.2 million years ago. Lucy was discovered in 1974 in Hadar, part of the Danakil Depression—one of the lowest points in Africa (155 meters below sea level) and one of the world's harshest climates, with summer temperatures consistently topping out at 48 degrees Celsius. At the time of Lucy's discovery, she was the oldest hominid unearthed. Twenty years later, in 1994, another team of scientists discovered "Ardi" in Aramis, in the middle Awash of the Afar desert. Ardi is the most complete skeletal find of the early hominids, and at 4.4 million years old was walking 1.2 million years earlier than Lucy. Human evolution continues to show its full scope in Ethiopia's Awash and Danakil regions, with discoveries made yearly.

Africa's third-highest mountain, Ras Dashen (4,543 meters), spikes in Ethiopia's Simien Mountains in the northwest, while the Ethiopian highlands form the largest continuous area of significant altitude (above 1,500 meters) in the African continent. Great mountain ranges spread throughout the country and shelter geological, zoological, and botanical diversity. Addis Ababa, Ethiopia's capital, sits 2,400 meters above sea level and is Africa's third-largest city. While close to 80 percent of Ethiopians live in the countryside, urbanization is increasing by 5 percent annually.

Geographically, Ethiopia is twice the size of France. With more than one hundred million people, Ethiopia is Africa's second most populous nation and the fourteenth most populous country in the world. Ethiopians face a sixty-four-year life expectancy (male and female averaged); women bear an average of five children. The Ethiopian calendar, based on the Coptic Calendar, is still used today, creating a seven- to eight-year gap between Ethiopia's year and the year according to the Georgian Calendar used predominantly throughout the rest of the world. The Ethiopian year consists of twelve months of thirty days, plus a thirteenth month of five or six days. Time is told in Ethiopia in twelve-hour increments, with one cycle from one to twelve reflecting dawn to dusk, and the second from dusk to dawn.

Historically, Ethiopia is thought to have been part of the ancient Land of Punt, a global trading center that thrived in 3500 BC; the country is also home to the four-thousand-year-old Ge'ez language, the precursor to both Amharic and Arabic. Here, too, the Axumite Kingdom ruled more than two thousand years ago, regulating trade between India and the Mediterranean. Axum legends claim that the Queen of Sheba considered Axum home and that the Ark of the Covenant has its final resting place in the region today. Beyond the legends, the ancient kingdom's might is plain to see in Axum's obelisks, called Stelae, one of which measures thirty-three meters tall and is considered the largest single block of stone humans have ever attempted to erect. It now lies in three pieces on the grounds of the Stelae Field, surrounded by more than 120 other such stones.

Christianity arrived in Ethiopia in the fourth century, and by the fifth century monasticism began to spread here. Christianity soon took physical root via dozens upon dozens of rock-hewn churches in Laibela and Tigray. Islam gained a presence in the seventh century, and today Harar, in eastern Ethiopia, is considered the fourth Holiest City of Islam. Judaism also has strong roots in Ethiopia, and the Beta Israel have lived throughout northern Ethiopia since pre-Christian times. Currently, the majority of Beta Israel live in Israel, the country. Today, Ethiopia is 60 percent Christian and 35 percent Muslim.

Ethiopia is home to the Solomonic Dynasty, an imperial bloodline dating back to King Solomon and the Queen of Sheba in 1000 BC and continuing until Emperor Haile Selassie's death, in 1975. Born Tafari Makonnen, Selassie was Ethiopia's Regent starting in 1916, and took over as Emperor in 1930. He was instrumental in Ethiopia's popular emergence onto the world stage in the mid-twentieth century. In 1923, Ethiopia joined the League of Nations. In 1930, Selassie was *Time's* Man of the Year; he presided at John F. Kennedy's funeral, and to this day is revered as Jesus incarnate by many Rastafari. Selassie governed Ethiopia in exile through the Italian occupation of 1936–1941, and returned to his home country with the help of the British in 1941. The emperor was the last to rule Ethiopia via a feudal system and was in power during the

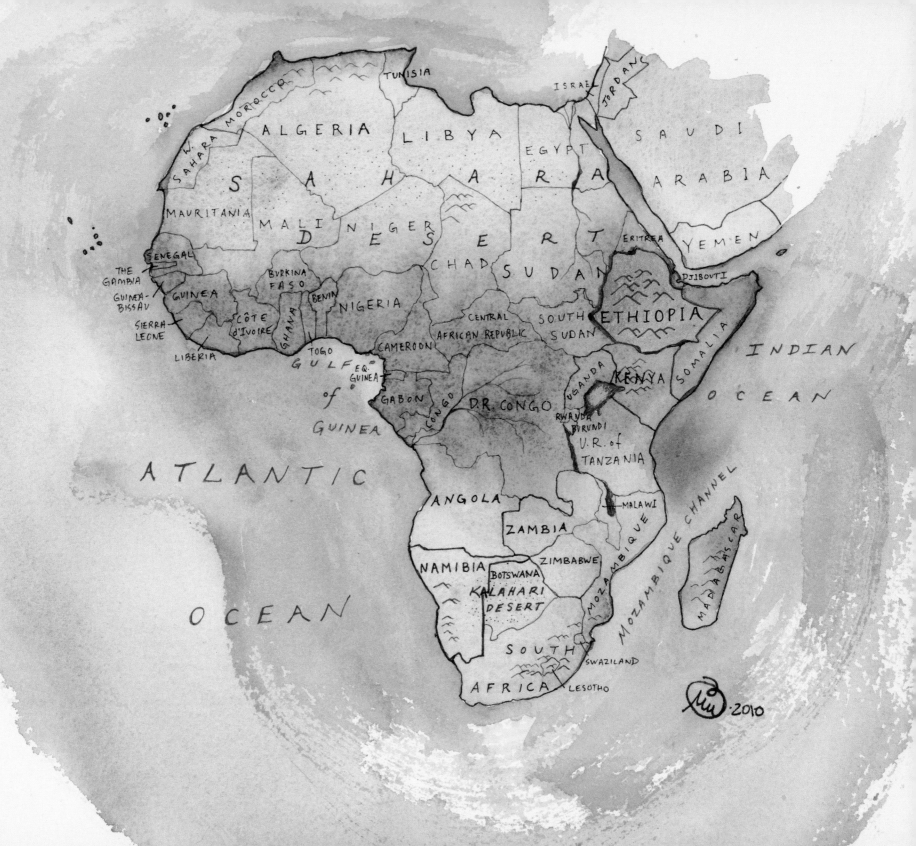

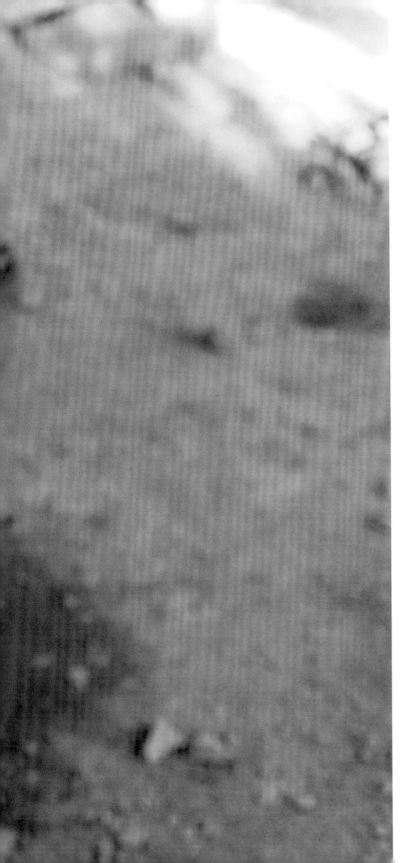

1972–74 famine that resulted in more than 40,000 deaths. In 1974, Emperor Selassie was ousted by the Derg, a communist military junta.

The Derg ended imperial rule in Ethiopia and replaced it with the "Red Terror," which ushered in a seventeen-year period of unrest, massacre, and violence under the governance of Mengistu Haile Mariam. The great famine of 1984, immortalized throughout the world by Live Aid and the song "We Are the World," took place during Mengistu's reign.

In 1991, a conglomerated group of rebels run by political leader Meles Zenawi overthrew the Derg. Zenawi, then chairman of the Tigrayan People's Liberation Front (TPLF), a rebel group in the northern province of Tigray, presided as prime minister of Ethiopia until his death in 2012. Under Zenawi's leadership, Ethiopia became both more stable and more beset by troubles, a trend that continues today. Ethiopia is a bastion for Western aid, and is currently receiving the largest amount of foreign aid in Sub-Saharan Africa. It is the only Christian-majority country in the greater Horn of Africa, surrounded by Islamic Somalia, Kenya, South Sudan, and Sudan. Zenawi and his successor, Hailemariam Desalegn, had complicated tenures, including pressure points like contested elections, increased separatist activity, press-freedom viola-tions, mounting human-rights abuses, and an ongoing poverty crisis. But they also brought about many improvements, including a 70 percent reduction in child mor-tality, increased focus on education, and advancements in healthcare. In 2017, the International Monetary Fund and the World Bank heralded Ethiopia as Africa's economic growth leader, and the country is well on its way to its goal of being a middle-income country, as classified by the World Bank, by 2025. In March 2018, Ethiopia moved closer toward these goals with the election of Abiy Ahmed, a reform-minded prime minister being heralded internationally as both a progressive and unifying leader who, since he took office, has been actively advancing his agenda. Ethiopia, today, is defined by change, and its future is charting a course for the same.

In summary, Ethiopia has a grand legacy as Africa's oldest independent country. Many cite this fact as the touchstone of her immense national pride. This pride is unmistakable, as is Ethiopian hope. No factual summary can ever encapsulate the verve of Ethiopia; at best, it can give a bit of context to the country and her people.

Sisters at a well in Harar.

ETHIOPIAN DUALITY

It's October 2009, and my flight arrives early into Addis Ababa. Long before deplaning, I am oriented by the smell pouring through the plane's passenger door. It's both thick and crisp, as if of life itself, mixed with wood smoke and frankincense. It's been two years since I've set foot in Ethiopia, though I am here daily in my mind (and work—as a writer). Within an hour, I'm riding through Addis, picking out new buildings and roads. A new hotel sits around every corner—corners that used to house construction sites anchored by clusters of tied-together sticks and buttressed by wobbly log ramps that I would look at and wonder, *What if?* What if the concrete poured into rough-edged joints became smoothed-over corners? What if the buckling floors, seen easily through the framing and bowed just enough to make you feel a sense of movement as you zipped past in a "blue devil"—an Addis taxi—became foundations for a room? Now they have; now they are. Traffic circles have replaced fifteen-pronged dirt-road intersections. Mobile phones are as omnipresent as the cows and goats that are herded through the streets from one exurban pasture to the next.

The following morning, I awake to bougainvillea. In Africa, you can always smell everything first—before you see it. I follow the scent to the botanical gardens, where I'll spend the morning. I count three BMWs as I walk. It used to be there were only six in the country, and within a week of living in Addis I knew them as well as any local. Now there are too many to count.

In my eyes, Addis (and Ethiopia) is in a better place than it was during my second and most recent prior visit, in 2007. But it is easy, I think, to return to Ethiopia and see progress; it is human to hope rather than to despair. Despair was all too familiar the first time I came here, in 2006. Nothing can prepare anyone for continuous exposure to human suffering. And so we see it, and then we look for what signals its amelioration. But really, it never leaves our consciousness.

I leave the gardens and walk past a little boy still huddled in sleep against a concrete fence rimmed with broken glass. He looks peaceful in slumber, or I want him to be peaceful, but really, I don't know anything about him. I think he is four, but he could be eight. Malnutrition is rampant in Ethiopia, even in the prospering capital, and can stunt the growth of any human exposed to its malign influence. I walk away from the boy, telling myself that he will be there the next day, that I will help him somehow. But I never see him again. Instead, for the weeks to come, his face peers out from the visage of every hungry child I see. And it flickers also in every child I see laughing and singing and loved by his or her family.

Writing about Ethiopia is a textual tightrope walk. There is beauty next to desolation, opportunity beside devastation, abundance encroached upon by profound scarcity. To write about Ethiopia's glories without addressing her struggles would be disingenuous. To write about the struggles, without an eye for hope, would be disrespectful. This dilemma is further complicated when writing about coffee—the crop that creates a livelihood for a quarter of the population and accounts for 60 percent of Ethiopia's foreign earnings.

It's farmers and their families who tend this crop, and in Ethiopia they make the equivalent of between seven and forty-five cents per kilogram of coffee cherries. On the opposite side of the consumption chain, people pay anywhere between two and fifteen USD for a cup of coffee that used one twentieth of that kilogram (when taking into account weight reduction from drying and roasting). The intent of *Coffee Story: Ethiopia* is not to belabor this economic discrepancy, but neither is it to ignore it. Instead, the goal is to show the human side of coffee—the humanity surrounding coffee in all its forms—be it impoverished, wealthy, exhausted, inventive, ecstatic, exploited, or subject to the harshest realities. Stories unify all of these possibilities. My hope is for these stories to turn statistics into people. That was my goal when I began my research, and was a consistently verbalized goal of those whom I interviewed: *Tell my story. Appreciate my coffee. Hear my name.*

Preceding pages: **Lake Tana.**
Opposite: **Sidamo.**
Overleaf: **Running at dawn with Addis Ababa in the background.**

THE RIGHT TO TELL A STORY

What would you say if someone knocked on your front door and asked you to tell them a story? What if they asked you what coffee meant to you? Or to your great-grandmother? Or if they asked what coffee meant to you, behind closed doors, in your religion and beliefs? Would you allow them inside your home? Would you share your life?

Telling other people's stories is a process laden with danger and beauty. At a humanistic level, storytelling is the heart of communication. How, then, do you engage in that heart and do it responsibly when you become the conduit for the tales of others?

One day in November 2009, in the mountains of eastern Ethiopia, I interviewed a farmer for twenty minutes about what coffee meant to him and his family. I asked him every leading question I knew, interview tactics that had produced results for years. But not with this man. Each time I tried a new tack, his answer was the same: "Coffee is what I grow. It's what makes me and my family money." I left feeling I had failed to gain his trust. It was not until that evening, looking over my notes, that I realized the man's answers might have been precisely that: his answers.

The soul of this book presupposes a deep, rich connection with coffee that transcends the physical bean itself. But to accurately write about coffee in Ethiopia, I first had to understand that sometimes coffee is just a crop. The surprising and complex narratives were gifts when I found them. But to appreciate them, I had to equally appreciate the simplicity of a plant that creates revenue being nothing more than that—a money-earner. Furthermore, I had to let stories be stories, and to let go of my need for them to always be about something more.

At the heart of anthropological discourse is an understanding that the observer brings his or her experience to any observation. So-called popular anthropology—magazine articles, coffee-table books, etc.—oftentimes strays from the rules demanding objective, responsible representation. Ironically, popular anthropology interacts with a far greater portion of the world's population than academic anthropology and therefore creates a bigger wake with its interpretations. How, then, was I to represent an "other" without being paralyzed by my awareness of that wake? As I wrote, I continually challenged myself to be accountable to academic-anthropological standards within the construct of a popular-anthropological project. I did so as a writer who studied anthropology just long enough to earn a bachelor's degree and to leave school with the unanswered questions that quickly propelled me into a life of adventure and journalistic expression.

In the pages that follow, I have tried my best to share stories the way they were told. Whenever possible, I use the names of the people with whom I spoke. I've followed Ethiopian custom and primarily identified people with their first name, occasionally preceded with Ato, Woizero, or Woizerit to connote a place of respect in their respective community. Often, people would not give me their names; at other times, it was difficult to record the names. The photographs have similar histories. The captions are interpretations of what was happening in the moment. Robert Gordon, who specializes in visual anthropology, makes the case for "visual literary," a more accurate representation of the entire photographic process. As he writes: "The stock-in-trade of cultural anthropology is the analysis of 'sociocultural context'—in making sense of the customs of the ubiquitous other. Yet we do not apply it to our own efforts at constructing ways (customs) of perceiving others."

Photographs are at the core of this construction—and of this book. I have thus attempted via the writing to offer a fluid interpretation of that which the camera lens captured, and that which it missed. Ultimately, no one can tell you what anyone else is thinking. But if we let that structure govern our communication, we would be silent cohabitators of our world. I would rather live in a shared world.

In the pages that follow, you will find stories presented as they were told, stories that stand alone, and stories with both storyteller and listener as integral characters. There is a playfulness inherent to gathering tales, though that playfulness is often removed from the final product in an effort at creating a relevant text. I believe in moving toward an amalgamated view of shared storytelling, in which everyone involved in the telling and hearing has a presence on the page. It's fitting to make this case in a book about Ethiopian coffee that argues for coffee as synonymous, ultimately, with connection.

Woizero Fatuma Siti and Majka Burhardt
inside Woizero Fatuma's home in Harar.

15

The outskirts of Addis Ababa.

COFFEE, SIMPLY

Bright-red succulent cherries hold a tandem treasure that fuels much of the developing world's economy. Inside the thick skin of a coffee berry lie two identical halves of a coffee seed, paired with each other for the majority of their lives. For those who grow coffee, as much time is spent with the bean as a whole as it is with the seeds as individuals. For those who consume coffee, most only come into contact with individual seeds—either roasted to a fine mahogany or ebony, or still "green" with distinctive varietal flecks or the hue of processing. Coffee has infinite ways of transitioning from a seed on a tree stem to a drinkable infusion. Ethiopia practices them all.

Put most simply, coffee processing is the transition from a lush cherry to a single dried green coffee seed. After farmers pick the cherry from the branch, a decision is made if the cherry is to be dried as-is in the sun (also called natural or dry process) or if the outer fruit will be removed and the seed sent to dry (also called washed process). Semi-washed or pulped natural process involves removing the skin of the cherry prior to drying, while leaving some of the sweet mucilage to dry with the seeds. No matter which process, all coffee seeds reach an eventual stage in which they have been dried to a target moisture content and freed from their outer layers. So-called "green coffee," if stored well, can remain preserved for export and roasting for up to one year or more. Once roasted, coffee deteriorates in quality within ten to fourteen days. Once ground, aroma escapes and coffees degrade within hours. Once brewed, the volatile aromatic compounds within good coffee are best enjoyed immediately.

Throughout Ethiopia, you'll see family plots, cooperatives, corporate mills, and private farms all working year-round to grow, harvest, process, and protect their coffee. Because large-scale industrialization was absent in Ethiopian coffee processing in the 1970s and '80s (due to the socialist/military control of the Derg), coffee cultivation remained more individualized. This was the crescendo of an era of large-scale industrialization in the world's other coffee-production centers, particularly in South America. That Ethiopia kept its micro-processing focus was an inadvertent decision, born from the rugged landscape and political context rather than made as a coffee-focused choice. Ethiopia's vast and varied coffee landscapes and thousands of unique botanical varieties are thus some of its greatest assets—they've for centuries protected the immense diversity of flavor and processing methods. The result today is fine coffee emerging—from a land of plenty—for boutique-coffee appreciation: a movement that creates appreciation of flavor and the culture surrounding it.

Opposite & below: **Picking the best cherry in Yirgalem.**
Overleaf: **Semeon Abay, Addis Ababa.**

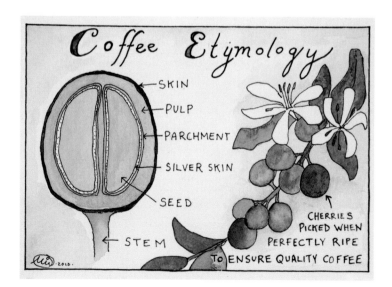

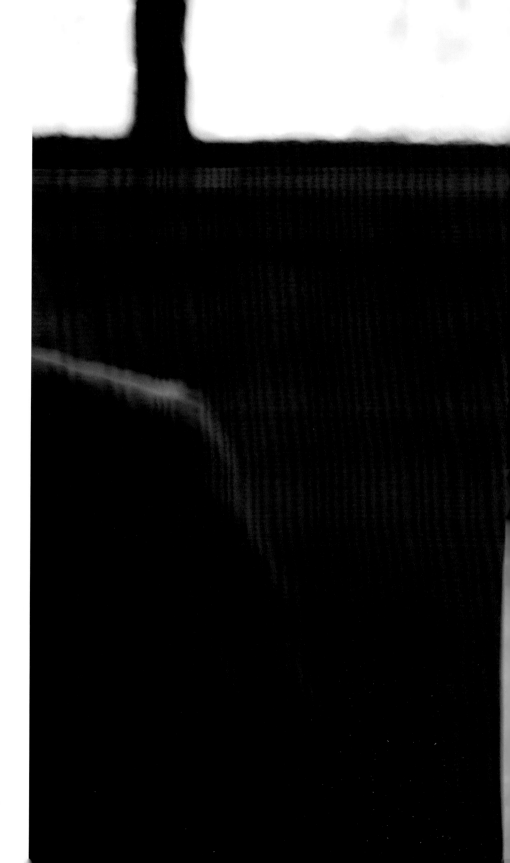

COFFEE STORY: ETHIOPIA

TRUTH IN CEREMONY

"How do you say, 'coffee ceremony' in Amharic?" I ask my friend Semeon Abay one morning in Addis.

"You don't."

I furrow my brow.

"Really," Semeon says. "You just say, '*Buna. Buna tetu!*'—'Come for coffee!'"

It's 8:30 a.m. and we are in a coffee shop in the heart of the Arat Kilo neighborhood in Addis. Balzac quotes on the importance of coffee line the walls. The heat radiating off the roaster will soon accent the heat of the day. The shop is divided between an Ethiopian cultural coffee tableau—where a young woman roasts, grinds, and brews coffee in the "traditional" Ethiopian way—and a mechanized coffee bar with a four-group espresso station. When customers arrive, they can choose to have the Ethiopian Coffee Ceremony or a cup of coffee. But to Semeon, these choices are the same thing.

Throughout Ethiopia, people often drink their coffee in three stages, bringing the same portion of coffee grounds to a boil for each stage and enjoying first a strong cup, known as *abol* or *awol*, and then progressively weaker brews called *tona, tala, thani,* and a final round, *baraka*. Having coffee in this manner takes time, and creates a space of community and conviviality. The naming of it as a *coffee ceremony* dates back to the early nineteenth century. Today, Ethiopians of diverse cultural backgrounds will call their own coffee drinking a "coffee ceremony," using the English term, advertising it on billboards and mentioning it when you come to their homes. The ceremonial aspects are many and not to be discounted for their origins, but the actual naming importance bestowed by the word *ceremony* is absent in the true expression of, simply, *buna*.

"When I was a kid," Semeon tells me, "my job was to tell the others, 'Buna tetu!' I would run to the neighbor's house and tell them to come. All of the women would arrive and drink coffee—they even had their own cups at each other's houses. My mother would host, or her friend would, or another friend. Three times a day, every day."

The specifics by which coffee is drunk change throughout Ethiopia. For Semeon, in Addis, he always had three cups of coffee each time he drank it at home. When he was little, he often would not make it through all the cups: "The children drink it for the sugar," he says, "the adults for the caffeine." In *Coffee Story: Ethiopia*, we'll explore micro-adaptations in the significance of the cup order, the symbolism of conversation vis-à-vis the timing in the three-stage process, and additional connections to ritual as they arise in the different regions.

The primary ceremony process is detailed in the section on Kaffa, beginning on page 29. Adaptations, like any variation of anything in Ethiopia, appear everywhere.

Opposite: **Abshire Seman Nuri prepares coffee in Hirna.**
Overleaf: **Derbe Menana, Amaro Mountains.**

COFFEE ETYMOLOGY IN FACT & MYTH

Because of its naming history and its biological home, coffee's origin claims are often conflated. The Kaffa region has become understood to be the birthplace of coffee—a correct biological fact, but an incorrect linguistic supposition. The ease of translation, onomatopoeically, of Kaffa to *coffee* fostered this semantic leap, first made by the Scottish explorer James Bruce in 1790 and then again by the Italian geographer Antonio Cecchi in 1888.

Kaffa more deeply informs coffee's etymology thanks to the story of Khaldi, a goat herder or monk (depending on the version) who saw his goats energized by a foreign plant later discovered to do the same for humans. Paul Merab, a Georgian physician who traveled in Ethiopia in the 1900s, reported that he could find no one in Ethiopia who'd heard Khaldi's tale, though the rest of the world told it with certainty at the time. Over the course of a century, the power of that story has made it commonplace, so much so that today in Ethiopia I have heard it from elders, schoolchildren, coffee farmers, and even those who've never seen a raw coffee bean. In every story, Khaldi lives in Kaffa, and Kaffa creates coffee.

The term *coffee* is actually an adaptation of the Arabic *qahwa*, a wine made from coffee's brew in the seventeenth century in Yemen. Carl Linneaus, the Swedish creator of taxonomy, named the coffee plant *Coffee arabica* in 1753 based on this association, though evidence points to the use of the word *buna* to identify the plant more than a century before it became *Coffee arabica*. The misnaming of Arabica is a sore subject with many Ethiopians; as Gezahegn Berecha Yadessa, a professor at Jimma University in Southern Ethiopia, says, it has remained unchanged because "We don't have the power and publicity to get the name of our coffee back."

What Ethiopia does have, and has always had, is a consistent name for the berry and drink that crosses Amharic, Omotic, Cushitic, and several Semitic languages: buna, *bunn*, or *bun*. Even in Arabic, *bunn* is used to refer to the bean, and as the academic Rita Pankhurst so aptly pointed out, *bunni* is the Arabic term for "brown"—the color of the bean when roasted. This consistency has become the singularly strongest piece of evidence for coffee's origin in Ethiopia. It's only fitting that everywhere you travel today in Ethiopia, buna is what people offer from their stoops, their stores, and their homes to welcome a foreigner or a friend.

Derbe Menana, Amaro Mountains

KAFFA

Perhaps it's fitting that the land most commonly associated with coffee's genetic roots was once a kingdom unto itself. From the fourteenth century until 1897, Kaffa maintained its sovereignty. Then Emperor Menelik II eventually dissolved the kingdom during his war with Kaffa and several other southern independent states. Today, the dense, forested land— an impenetrable highland removed from the rest of the world—still bespeaks an earlier epoch of absolute provincial power and imposing, two-meter-tall kings. Kaffa was the ideal place for coffee to lie in wait for its discovery.

"Have you been to the kingdom of Kaffa?" an Ethiopian man once asked me at the Denver International Airport.

I had told him I was writing a book on coffee. "How could I not?" I answered.

I entered Kaffa within my first three days in Ethiopia, in 2006. We left Addis in a jetlagged fog, following a checkerboard dirt and asphalt road that led us away from the buildings and traffic and soon twisted through golden-green chickpea fields that reflected the sunset over the Awash River. Kaffa was up ahead and then, suddenly, all around us.

Today, Kaffa is a label for an ethnic division of Ethiopia split between Oromiya and the Southern Nations, Nationalities and People's Region. Jimma, the largest city in western Ethiopia, is at Kaffa's physical, intellectual, and agricultural crossroads. The city is marked by its castle, airport, university, and a convergence of roads filled with coffee-laden trucks. Spreading westward from Jimma, tiny towns interlace with yet smaller villages via rough dirt roads interrupted by coffee mills. Long, elevated drying beds are opened to the rays of the sun by day, and then tightly bound in yellow plastic by night. In the dark countryside, the only lights are the mills, magnified as they reflect off the yellow bundles.

Just saying "Kaffa" invokes a connection to coffee (see page 24 for etymological details). Although many areas within Kaffa claim the physical home of the first coffee tree, most scientists agree that coffee originated in the highland border country between Ethiopia and Sudan. Judging by the tenacity of the legends, Kaffa is clearly coffee's conceptual home: the main origination story of Khaldi and his goats has always been sited here.

Throughout the twentieth century, several resettlement efforts moved people to Kaffa from Ethiopia's less-fertile regions. A larger population creates a larger strain on the natural resources, and coffee has been both a winner and a loser in this equation. Coffee trees do not make good building or burning materials, but they rely upon other, more robust trees to create the much-needed shade for proliferation. Coffee's saving grace is its value. Recent worldwide acceptance of Kaffa as home to all the world's *Coffee arabica* has created a vested interest in saving the coffee that grows in the heartland.

Homes in Kaffa.

BACKYARD BOUNTY

This morning, we borrow shade from thick enset leaves bordering the dirt path. Enset, also called false banana, is an Ethiopian staple and one of its most effective measures against hunger—one root bundle can provide up to forty kilograms of food. The leaves reach up to four meters tall and two meters wide; today, they canopy us in green when we need it. Coffee peeks from the ensets' understory and spills forth from every vista.

We meet a farmer walking out of his home with a half-kilogram basket of red cherries. He's picked them from the trees surrounding his house.

"There's a story of coffee starting in Choche," I say, "not far from here. Do you know it?"

"Yes," he says.

"Can you tell it to us?"

"All the people who know it are dead."

"Really?" I ask.

He nods, machete in one hand, coffee basket in the other. He walks away before I can get his name. Soon he's disappeared into the coffee forest.

This is the land of wild coffee, coffee not planted but simply growing where birds deposit the seeds. The trees here differ even within a foot of each other in terms of branch height, leaf size and configuration, and berry shape. If one family picks their coffee from a set of trees, it's usually mixed in at a mill with the coffees of countless other families. But at home, that family drinks *their* coffee, which might be the best man has ever tasted. It's possible here in Kaffa with its labyrinth of coffee options extending into ancient forests, forests that hold individual coffee varieties still unknown to the outside world for their uniqueness.

Mankira.

COFFEE STORY: ETHIOPIA

TRADITIONAL COFFEE FARMING AS SEEN IN THE KAFFA FOREST, ETHIOPIA

PICK WRAP CARRY DRY HULL

TRADITIONAL COFFEE PROCESS

Throughout Ethiopia, people pick, process, and prepare coffee by hand for their own consumption. During coffee-harvest season, homes are constantly engaged in some stage of the harvest: picking, drying, hulling, sorting, and always—every day—roasting, grinding, and drinking. While everyone— women, men, and children—processes the raw coffee, it is customary for only women to prepare the drink.

Coffee is traditionally roasted on a flat metal pan atop a charcoal brazier. The beans are stirred with a long metal spatula with a curled end that more easily moves them about the pan. Incense (frankincense and myrrh resin) is often sprinkled on additional charcoal nearby to combine with the coffee

aroma. Some form of food, often qollo (roasted barley), is served while the coffee is roasted. Once roasted and cooled, the beans are ground by pounding them in a long, tubular wooden mortar. The grounds are then transferred into a heated jebena (an earthenware pot with a round belly) full of water. The jebena is set to brew with a grass cork to prevent evaporation. The coffee is now heated and cooled to individual preference, and soon distributed among small,

handle-less ceramic cups arranged on a squat tray called a rakabot or ganda. The coffee is poured through the jebena's thin spout high above the cups and doled out to those in attendance. Spices, butter, milk, and/or tennadum (a sprig of rue) are added depending on regional, tribal, and personal preference.

FROM KAFFA TO COFFEE, & BACK AGAIN

Ato Abera Kebede is a Muslim man with a Christian name. He meets us outside his house, a half-dozen kilometers and four hairpin turns from one of the claimed loci of the original coffee trees near Choche. When I ask Ato Abera for the story he knows about coffee, he tells me about Khaldi, who, with a Muslim twist, becomes Khaled.

Khaled was a researcher who lived in a village here in Kaffa. One day, the village goats started to make a great ruckus. It was Khaled who noted that the goats were eating coffee, and who, the next morning, collected the berries, roasted them, pounded them with a rock, and brewed the first coffee.

Khaled was an industrious scholar and spent many nights struggling to stay awake, until he discovered coffee. From then on, Ato Abera explains, spreading his arms wide to encompass the others listening, "we all drank coffee."

I tell Ato Abera I very much like this story of Khaldi/Khaled. He tells me he is not finished telling it.

Khaled, according to Ato Abera, next dried the berries and put them in a makeshift bag, and then took them to Arabia. When he arrived, people wanted to know what he was carrying and from whence he'd brought it.

"I brought it from Kaffa," Khaled said.

"What is the name?" they asked.

"There is no name," he replied.

Together, the Arabs and Khaled named it the Kaffa drink. That, Ato Abera tells me, is why Kaffa is *kaffe* and now coffee.

Kaffa's claim to coffee etymology is undisputed in the kingdom. Outside Kaffa, however, other theories—some scientific, some folkloric—place a lower premium on this connection. Regardless, the linguistics have been adopted by many a traveler and historian. For variations, see pages 24 and 60.

Above: **Coffee seedlings.**
Opposite: **Evening in Jimma.**

KAFFA FROM THE ARCHIVES

Few written accounts exist of Kaffa before the end of the nineteenth century, when foreigners first reached the kingdom. Lore places coffee with the Queen of Sheba in the tenth century BC, and supposition stands that coffee was used far earlier than academic accounts would suggest. In the late nineteenth century, the people of Kaffa (Kafichios) were reported to brew coffee with spices and discard the husks, as well as to serve coffee cherries roasted whole and soaked in melted butter with honey.

Where the coffee habits of the Kafichios came from is purely a matter of academic supposition. The Manjo, who inhabited the kingdom until the thirteenth century, were hunter-gatherers and most likely ate coffee cherries and used them in some form. Cattle, however, were not introduced into the kingdom until after the Manjo rule, and thus the addition of butter or milk would not have been possible before then. What is clear is that by the seventeenth century, the Kafichios had passed on their preparation style of coffee with butter, honey, and herbs to the Oromo when the latter, at that time, migrated to the area. The Busani, the only ethnic group along southwestern Ethiopia's borderland to cultivate coffee, are said to have originally come from Kaffa.

Jimma.

A BEAN FOR YOUR HAND

Deep in Kaffa, when a man wishes to marry a woman, he offers her family his coffee. During Nika, the time when the man's family travels to the woman's family to ask for the woman's hand on the suitor's behalf, a portion of the groom's coffee land is given to the bride's family. The groom and his family commit to continuing to tend the land; once the couple is married, the bride's family will reap the benefits of the coffee sales from that parcel.

Ato Abera and his wife tell me this story. I ask her if her family received coffee from her husband's family, and she nods in reply.

"Is there anything else you want to know?" Ato Abera asks.

"Is there anything you want to know from me?" I ask.

"How is all of this useful for Ethiopia?" he wonders.

Together, we look around. Earlier, the twenty people gathered around us had all nodded as Ato Abera told me that coffee is what clothes his people and educates his children. Everyone, now, awaits my answer.

RESEARCH IN THE HEARTLAND

Scientists, researchers, agronomists, and trained quality-control engineers work together at the Jimma Research Center to study Ethiopia's prime asset: the world's greatest concentration of coffee biodiversity, found in Kaffa's deep forests. As the professor of agriculture Gezahegn Berecha Yadessa explained during an interview, "If this forest is threatened, it is not only a challenge for Ethiopian coffee business, but also world business. More than 70 percent of coffee production in the world comes from this variety."

The Jimma Research Center is working to catalog and preserve each morphologically different type of coffee based on leaf color, productivity, etc. To date, they've catalogued more than five thousand such accessions, and expect that twice as many remain to be chronicled.

Preparing coffee at the Jimma Research Center: removing parchment and weighing beans for sample roasting. In a nearby room, a white Formica table holds coffee samples from all of Ethiopia's regions. Taste characteristics are assigned to each. Cuppers here are internationally certified, and they grind, roast, and taste each small lot of coffee to match the quality and the authenticity to a particular region.

QUALITY FROM THE SOURCE

Abrar Sualeh is the head researcher and cupper at the Jimma Research Center. Wearing a long white coat, he governs the roasting, tasting, and sorting in a clean, airy lab surrounded by hectares of experimental coffee gardens. Today, like any other day, his colleagues roll coffee beans between their fingers to remove the parchment. They build one-hundred-gram sample piles to roast and cup. No one yet knows if this accession will be approved for release to farmers. The lab has five certified coffee cuppers who grade the taste, clarity, acidity, aroma, and body of each possible coffee. When the research station opened, in 1971, the goal was to find the most drought- and disease-resistant coffee plants with the highest yield, and make them available throughout the country. In the beginning, it took an average of twenty years to release a new coffee variety. Then, in the early 1990s, as the new coffees were planted across Ethiopia, the scientists realized an error: coffees that grow well in one part of the country could fail in another. Thus farmers who had uprooted their indigenous coffee trees to plant the new, government-sanctioned high-yield trees ended up either without any coffee cherries or with cherries that had lost all regional distinctiveness. A Yirga Cheffe no longer tasted like a Yirga Cheffe. Realizing the loss, the center in 1994 turned its attention to regional offices that would produce region-specific coffees retaining the local qualities.

Today, a coffee release takes eight years, and in 2009 fourteen coffees were released. The new seedlings were available at government nurseries for those planting in the specific regions.

THE KAFFA OX, A FIRE, OTHER STORIES OF ORIGIN

Tamagn Tedesse does not tell a story of Khaldi or goats; he tells of an ox and a farmer. The legend is such: One night, a farmer noticed that one of his oxen smelled different than before. He smelled good. His smell even made the farmer hungry. The next day, the farmer followed the ox into the field and watched as the beast ate the leaves of a plant. The farmer later went to inspect the leaves and realized that they, not the ox, were what smelled so good. Soon after, the farmer's community ate the leaves, and eventually the cherries.

After Ato Tamagn tells us about the ox, he immediately launches into another story.

"In the forest," he says, "there was once a fire, and the coffee plants burned with it. The community smelled something different. They wondered about the unique smell, and they identified the plant with the sweet smell. Afterwards, they started planting coffee, roasting it, and drinking it."

Stories shared, he pauses and then continues: "This," he says, stomping his foot, "is the place where coffee was first tasted."

STARTING YOUNG

In Kaffa, most children are not allowed to have coffee until they are four years old. Everyone I meet puts it this way. No one says that children *begin* drinking at four; instead, it is that they have been *limited* from it before that age. Children start with the diluted brew of the third round and quickly progress to the strong first cup.

Above: **Child in Gonder.**
Opposite: **Tamagn Tedesse in Kaffa.**

COFFEE STORY: ETHIOPIA

rsity Conservation IBC
Field Genebank

· Altitude -
· Area -

Forty kilometers from the Jimma Research Center, a faded four-by-
two-meter billboard welcomes you to the "Birthplace of coffee." We
miss the road, and the billboard, on the first pass. The second time,
we join a line of cows and sheep, making our way down a dirt road
canopied by leafy trees to the Institute of Biodiversity Conservation.
It rests by itself, gated off and guarded, a tantalizing preserve of Ethiopia's agricultural bounty.

COFFEE'S USES

COFFEE TEA
In Kaffa, as in most of Ethiopia, coffee tea, a brew from coffee leaves, is also consumed. Here it is called *chemo*. The leaves are gathered and lightly roasted, added to water or milk, and boiled for an infusion. Chemo is traditionally spiced with ginger and berbere (hot pepper).

BUNA KELEMA
At a Kaffa wedding, guests indulge in Buna Kelema, a porridge of roasted coffee cherries mixed with butter and salt. They eat the mixture with a spoon. Traditional Kafichios roasted the leaves, crushed them, and prepared a refreshing infusion spiced with pepper.

BUNA BESSO
In southwest Ethiopia, coffee is often ground and mixed with barley, called Buna Besso.

STOMACH SAVIOR
Upset stomachs are common throughout Ethiopia, and a time-tested medicine is two spoonfuls of ground coffee mixed with honey.

TRAVELING ENERGY
In the late 1800s, many Oromo took to carrying energy balls of coffee and butter. The coffee would be roasted, pulverized, and rolled with butter to form an apple-sized orb, and then stored in a leather bag for travel.

Preceding spread: **Early morning in Kaffa.**
Right: **Spider suspended in web between branches of wild coffee tree, Kaffa.**
Opposite: **Farmer in Sidamo.**

ABADIR

In Kaffa, and much of Ethiopia, the coffee tree occasionally is called *abadir*. We meet a man who explains that a sheik named Abadir brought the plant here, which is why the tree bears his name. When we say that others have told us that coffee is from Kaffa, and was not brought here, the man shrugs.

"I don't know how coffee got here. I will not lie," he says.

This man's name is Ato Girma Wendafrash—when he tells us his name, he tells us Wendafrash means "he who produces only boys."

"Is this true?" we ask.

Ato Girma cracks a sly smile and turns away, saying nothing more.

HARAR

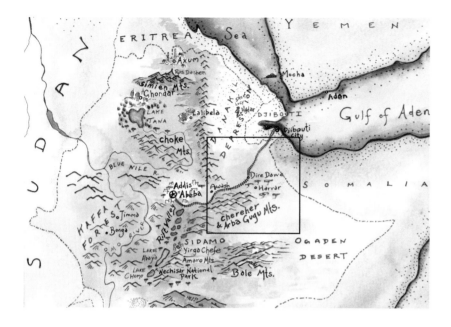

Acamel train stretches along the line of single-track railroad running east from Addis Ababa. There are eighteen camels in sight—eight ungainly young ones punctuating ten regal elders. The camels tower above the acacia trees, the beasts second in height only to the mountains cradling the lumbering valley through which they walk. Fantale Mountain (2,514 meters) engulfs the northern view. Fantale's top is missing—last blown off in 1928—and the conical massif reveals the volcanic underpinnings of the Rift Valley.

Today, we are crossing the Great Rift, heading east, on the way to Harar. To get there, we follow a paved road that loops lazily next to the railroad tracks. More travelers soon join the camels; the tracks take the road's place as the area thoroughfare. It's been three years since the last train. The railway was a joint French/Somali/Ethiopian effort launched in the 1890s that sought to modernize Ethiopian transportation, with current-day efforts seeking to revitalize the tracks. For now, the road and tracks cut across a land bridge on Lake Matahara, the easternmost Rift Valley lake. Hand-spun white cotton *netala* shawls and factory-produced tank tops from Asia share drying space on the iron rungs of the abandoned track. Shirtless men crouch next to the lakeshore, scrubbing their bodies and their clothes, while children submerge fully

in its water. Other people, post-wash, dry out on basalt and limestone boulders. The desire to rest here is strong—it is the last land that's clearly bountiful with vegetation and water before Awash National Park, a 900-square-kilometer arid landscape to the east.

Ten kilometers east of Lake Matahara, the land is utter desert. Early morning or late at night, the warthogs, anubis baboons, and beisa oryx flood the land, while lions, leopards, jackals, and hyenas prowl the gloom. Midday, it's abandoned save for us. Hot springs lie just out of sight. The road and the railroad continue their slash through the apparent desolation, as gentle, rounded topography beckons to the north, suggesting all we cannot see.

To drive anywhere in the heat of the Ethiopian day demands much of the traveler. Everything is parched and desolate, with the only succulent relief offered by an occasional roadside cluster of Sodom apple trees. Their softball-sized bright-green fruit is full of poisonous fibers, but the tree's presence signals life, as the roots shoot straight into unseen water veins. Local Afar people make their huts from the branches of the Sodom apple trees, their homes low and curved as dictated by the branch lengths.

This unwelcoming expanse explains much of the geographic separation of eastern Ethiopia from the central heartland. Our destination is Hararge, also called Harari, the province named for the ancient city of Harar. Founded between the seventh and ninth centuries, Harar is often referred to as the "fourth Holiest City of Islam," after Mecca, Medina, and Jerusalem. In 1887, Harar was incorporated into greater Ethiopia, thus ending the self-rule legacy of seventy-two emirs. The forty-second emir, Nur, established the now-infamous wall around the labyrinthine city.

Inside and outside the walled city, coffee cultivation has reigned in Harar for the past five centuries. Harar was the trading hub between the Red Sea, the Indian Ocean, and the extensive Ethiopian heartland. Coffee originated in Kaffa, but coffee trade developed in Harar. The Muslim city provided direct links to the Arab world, and propelled buna along its historic course and into the greater world by the end of the fifteenth century.

Preceding spread: **Harar daybreak.**
Opposite: **Woman in Sofi.**

THE AFAR

The Afar are a nomadic group that ranges from the desert triangle formed between Ethiopia, Eritrea, and Somalia down through the arid landscape into Hararge. Afar people create a drink similar to the coffee-leaf tea of the Harari, but often use all the components in the tea—leaves, husks, and beans. Afar men wear Kufi caps and cotton sarongs, and often strap Kalashnikovs to their shoulders. Noble warriors, pastoral, and fiercely protective of their lands, the Afar were often portrayed as erratically war hungry in twentieth-century Western travel literature. The Afar's waste-nothing coffee practice bespeaks the tenacity and resourcefulness required to live in the harsh environments where they thrive.

COFFEE ON THE MARCH

An account from the 1870s by the Earl of Mayo describes how Ethiopian Muslims drank coffee on the march. The unroasted berries, he explains, were placed on a mat and combined with wood ash. The mat would then be rolled and shaken to gradually roast the coffee. The Muslims used stones to grind the coffee into a powder, which was then placed in a jebena to be boiled. Mayo himself called the process a "ceremony," and noted that it was the most important time of day for the Muslim marchers.

Sodom apples along the road to Harar.

COFFEE FROM ETHIOPIA TO THE WORLD

Harar's combination of trading fortitude and geographical position led to the naming of coffee as *coffee*. As you'll recall, *qahwa*, an Arabic word first used for wine and then for the brew made from coffee beans, is the accepted etymological root of *coffee*. The exact year in which coffee left Ethiopia and traveled to Yemen is unknown. Some speculation cites the transfer occurring during the Aksumite invasion of South Arabia in the sixth century. Regardless, by the early 1500s, coffee (prepared by infusion) was well known in Yemen and throughout the Islamic world, though often associated with ceremony, religion, and wealth. By the end of the sixteenth century, coffee had traveled beyond Yemen via the port of Mocha, and the bean had again been renamed to reflect its most recent port of trade, not its origin. To this day, many people incorrectly recount a coffee origin story that centers on Mocha.

Coffee's popularity and value created an enduring system of slavery in eastern Ethiopia that was not fully eradicated until 1942. During the fourteenth and fifteenth centuries, the Oromo were forcibly brought to Hararge to work on the Harari farms. Over the centuries, most Oromos in Hararge, though traditionally Christian, converted to Islam. Oromo and Harari coffee traditions often exerted a mutual influence, and both cultures adopted a coffee-bean conservation strategy wherein the husks and leaves were consumed locally to maximize the export value of the beans to the outside world. Today, if you ask anyone in Hararge how she uses coffee, her answer will inevitably involve an overlapping story of Oromo and Harari use.

Opposite & right: **Scenes from Harar.**

ARID LUSHNESS

With a change of light, Ethiopia goes from desolate to beautiful. Today, this happens as we enter the Chercher Mountains. The railroad has twisted away from us and started its journey through twenty-two tunnels and viaducts into the mountains. Meanwhile, the asphalt roadbed climbs through layers of fields showcasing Ethiopia's agricultural bounties, crops still grown today exactly as they have been for centuries. Sisal shoots cover a west-facing slope, waiting to be harvested and made into the omnipresent coffee sacks seen throughout the world. Higher up, farmers gather sorghum stalks into bundles of five and six to create stable teepees in anticipation of the plant's top-heavy red flowers, soon to bloom. These mountains are ancient templates of human industriousness. Every surface suggests a time-honored practice of cultivation and the passage of untold human epochs. Soon we see endless rows of knee-high green bushes of *chat*—Ethiopia's hallucinogenic bounty and its ongoing point of agricultural controversy. For now, I take in the bright-green leaves in plant clusters in the fields, and soon see them in satchels on every woman, man, and child's back along the road. It is harvest time here. It is always harvest time. It has always been this way in Hararge. The hues of the land dictate which crop to pick, with sharp colors suggesting its respective ripeness and muted fields slumbering while they await their next rotation.

These mountains are milder cousins of the steeper peaks in other Ethiopian regions; here, the peaks are gentle mounds abutting ridgelines. Deep inside the hills, ancient paintings and rock carvings abound. Humid forests lie just to the south, but this swath surrounding the road is a study in carefully cultivated lushness amidst seeming desiccation.

Soon, the mountains drop into the plains, and the railroad comes back into sight with its decisive slice northwest away from Harar proper. Twenty years after its inception, the Ethiopian railway bypassed the city of Harar in favor of an easier and cheaper way through the highlands. Dire Dawa, "New Harar," was created along the tracks in its stead. Both cities thrum with the region's urban but ancient feel. In both, Harari people flood the streets at market time, with women filling the view in multicolored scarves that flicker like mirages. We started the day in a natural palette of grays, greens, and browns, and now find ourselves entering a manmade world of swirling magenta, ochre, and tangerine cotton and silk.

Chercher Mountains.

ROADSIDE COFFEE

Awash sits at the crossroads between the road north to the Afar Desert, the road east to Dire Dawa and Harar, and the road west to Addis. Its blankness belies a thriving market. We stop for gas, bread, and bananas.

"Buna?" asks a young girl, pressing a serving tray into our open car window.

She pours a steaming cupful to the rim and places a sprig of tennadum inside the cup to make the coffee overflow onto the saucer. The cup and saucer become one with the liquid, and I tilt both implements toward me, hesitating for a moment to inhale the sweet tennadum and smoky coffee, drinking straight through to the sugar at the bottom.

One hour in an unmarked café sees forty-five cups of coffee served. The waitstaff have sprinkled coffee grounds on the floor from the remnants of the morning's first espresso passes. This way, the flies are theoretically kept at bay, allowing more customers to linger for a second cup.

HARAR'S KAFFA

"Do you know the real story of Kaffa?" the scholar Amir Redwan asks me. Lounging in front of Ras Tafari's House, so named because the Emperor Haile Selassie (pre-coronation name: Ras [meaning Duke] Tafari) spent his honeymoon here inside the walled city, Redwan barely waits for me to incline my head before he shares the tale.

"Kaffa comes from Harar," Amir Redwan says, and then places a cigarette in his mouth, waits for a friend to bring a match in close, and draws in the smoke when it's lit. "Emir Nur, the forty-second emir of Harar, who built the wall? He named it."

When Amir Redwan talks, the cigarette flaps against his lips; nothing else on his face moves. He tells us that in the middle of the sixteenth century, Harar soldiers were fighting in what is now Kaffa. Emir Nur was leading the troops, and much blood was shed on both sides. One night, Redwan explains, Emir Nur had a dream that the war had to come to a conclusion. He woke up the next morning and declared, "*Kaffa!*"

"Do you know what *kaffa* means?" Amir Redwan asks me. The cigarette, drawn down, freezes while he waits. "Not this coffee connection," he says. His cigarette flaps three times. "But what it *means?*"

I shake my head.

"Nothing . . . in Amharic. But in Arabic, *kaf* means 'enough.' That is why he said, 'Kaffa!'—'Enough!'"

Cigarette finished, Amir Redwan reaches for another. "We named Kaffa," he concludes. "Harar started everything."

Right: Traditional Buna Sirri ceremony.
Opposite: Harar market.

SAVING THE BEAN FOR A ROOM OF LEAVES

My friend Teddy used to make an annual family trip in his father's Peugeot from Addis overland to Dire Dawa. When I ask him what he remembers most about his time in eastern Ethiopia, he tells me it's the kuti kela.

In much of Hararge, coffee—actual buna—is saved for religious occasions, births, marriages: the things to mark in life. The coffee leaves are what is used every day. Teddy's aunt, like many Hararis, had a room in her house reserved for storing leaves. Today, as well as then, the leaves are picked green and washed before being dried in the sun. Once dry, they are flash-roasted in a large skillet that is used to make enjera (Ethiopian flat bread)—"lightly, no oil," Teddy explains, "just to release the aroma." He inhales with the memory. The leaves are then stored in baskets and jars, and packed into a lofted room traditionally set to the right in a Harari house. A daily supply of leaves is brought down and brewed slowly with milk.

Each summer, when Teddy's family would pack for the long drive back to Addis, his aunt would give them a year's supply of leaves in jars. The Peugeot would smell like kuti kela on the drive home, and when they ran out—ten or twelve months later—they'd know it was time to return to Dire Dawa.

Opposite: Traditional Harari houses are customarily built of stone and clay, with an upstairs formerly reserved for the storage of coffee leaves, and now often a bedroom. Flat roofs provide ample coffee-bean-drying space, and the deep walls create a cool interior. Near the door, a set of spears is perched high on a wall in a wooden rack. They stand waiting at shoulder height: during peacetime, the tips face downward; during war, the handles are readily accessible.
Right: Morning in Dire Dawa.

BRANDING HARAR

A man at a coffee shop deep within the city walls tells me that Harar coffee is different.

"Why?" I ask.

"It's the only *Coffee arabica* in Ethiopia."

This man sets down a small cup with a flourish. I don't want to argue with him. For now, I choose to believe as I sip the brew's deep mocha and rich blueberry flavor.

Traditionally, Harar coffees were sun dried, though now washed coffees are equally common. Harar's connection to Arabia is still salient, and for many the husky flavor of Harar coffee is Ethiopian coffee.

MISSING BEANS

During the sixteenth and twenty-sixth days of Ramadan, Muslim Hararis gather for a ceremony marked by a porridge of coffee beans. Special, dark dried cherries are stewed in butter and sugar in an earthen pot and served atop a barley pancake: *sirri*. The sauce is thick and granular, and once dolloped on the pancake drips off the sides. Today, I am sharing the sirri with a group of women. It is not Ramadan, but they have agreed to show me their tradition.

We are all dressed in scarves, and behind my *fota* I take my first bite of *buna sirri*. I chew the coffee beans. My teeth click against each other, and I widen my eyes in surprise. The other women laugh, as they wait for me. I take another bite and put another cherry in my mouth. My teeth shoot straight through, again.

"Where is the bean?" I ask.

The women laugh. "*Wahber,*" they say. "Empty." One woman takes a bean between her fingers and pops it. In her hand is only air.

We drink kuti kela, coffee from Harar, and eat the sirri. Before long, my teeth ache from the sugar. I roll a few wahber beans in my mouth and try to politely remove them to look at later. Woizero Fatuma Siti notices.

"You want to see these beans?" she asks me later. In just moments, I am following her through the tight streets of inner Harar. I lose count after five turns and trust I will find my way back. Woizero Fatuma steps quickly over stone thresholds and through courtyards before darting down another narrow corridor. I trot behind her, watching for obstacles she steps over automatically. Soon she pauses before a blue door and turns to me. We have reached her home. Behind the home there is a storage cellar, and she pulls me inside it after her. A twenty-gallon sisal bag sits in the corner. It weighs less than a newborn baby. Woizero Fatuma again takes my hand and plunges it with hers deep into the bag. "Wahber," she says. We laugh, running our hands through these molecules of air.

The sack has five years' worth of wahber. In the market, I will see piles of the empty beans for sale for ceremony. Ramadan is almost a year away. Later, I will research and learn that these beans have coffee berry disease; they fall from the trees young and undeveloped—empty. Elsewhere in Ethiopia, they are rejected. Today, in Harar, they are royal.

Buna sirri, a Harari ritual meal involving a thick barley pancake topped with dried coffee cherries in butter.

COMPETING CROP

Two planes filled with fresh leaves of a legal stimulant leave every day from Dire Dawa to Djibouti. They are carrying chat. Many say they are also carrying away Ethiopia's future.

Some estimate that chat, also called *khat* and *qat*, has been part of Ethiopia for as long as coffee. Hararge has been the center of the Ethiopian chat trade because of the surrounding land's hospitable climate for growing the leaves, as well as the ease of trade with Arabia and now the rest of the world.

One legend tells a story of coffee and chat one day arguing about their importance to the Harari community. Says coffee, "I come once a year, but I give them houses, I give them weddings, and I give the community whatever they want."

Chat interrupts coffee: "You better stop there," chat says. "I support them with their daily expenses. Without that, they could not wait for you to come once a year."

Chat is a cash crop harvested daily in Ethiopia. While previously use was centered in the Arabian Peninsula, chat now can be legally found in England, the Netherlands, and Somalia, and illegally most everywhere else. Muslim culture has long incorporated chat into its leisure time, and recently people of all faiths have become indulgers. The drug creates a mild euphoria, sustained by the constant consumption of fresh leaves. Chat requires no processing and is at its most potent the moment it's picked. The Ethiopian economy has woven chat dependence into its taxation, transportation network, and quotidian life. Flatbed Isuzu trucks terrorize Ethiopian roadways as they, competing with the cargo planes, try to carry fresh chat inland to Addis, or to the borders beyond,

within an eight-hour window of its being picked. Chat tends to lose potency within forty-eight hours of being reaped, thus creating the rush for export.

High-quality chat can garner ten times the market price of coffee. It's no wonder that eastern Ethiopia has turned its fields over to the low-lying plant in the past two decades. As one man put it, with chat you plant in the morning and see the results in the afternoon.

The market value of chat, however, hides a greater social and environmental cost to Ethiopia. The mild stimulant is a constant green companion in the mouths of locals. Men, women, and children all chew the leaves, and some chat-riddled villages along the Addis-Harar road have even gone from being academic centers to chat-addled economic backwaters. Asbe Teferi (also called Chirro), a town that used to produce the most airline pilots per capita in Ethiopia, is now a place no one ever leaves. When we stop here for lunch, we see the oddest of sights: eight people in the restaurant's uniform sit at tables, looking only at each other when we ask where our food might be. Environmentally, chat creates acidic soil that precludes other crops from growing nearby. Entire lakes in Hararge are dry now, the water siphoned away for the chat. The surrounding houses now have satellite dishes instead of water.

Some say Addis makes $300,000/day from taxes on chat. Others ask if this is really Ethiopia's largest problem, given, for example, that there are more Ethiopian doctors in Washington, DC, than in all of Ethiopia. Either way, the chat crop is changing the Ethiopian landscape. In Hararge, it is life. The saving grace for the rest of the countryside, for now, is the relative difficulty of cross-country transport. As one coffee farmer in Sidamo tells me, he hopes Sidamo chat will never be good. "This way," he says, "Sidamo will be saved."

Haji Abdul Basitt in his home in Sofi.

HONORING THE ANCESTRAL

Harar is crammed and clustered into an area a mere kilometer square. Outside the city walls, the countryside sprawls multi-directionally, studded with farms that have long supported the city's eminence. Today, the surrounding landscape is parched, drawn down from chat cultivation. Accounts from the nineteenth century and turn of the twentieth century describe this landscape as one of Africa's most fertile. Coffee trees used to creep up to and through the city's walls. Today, the nearest coffee grows fifteen kilometers from the city, up in the hills of Sofi.

Sheik Sofi came to Harar from Medina with Sheik Abadi, the second emir of Harar. Sofi now rests in a stone shrine built in the ninth century. His descendants governed this area and soon produced, cultivated, and traded coffee. Haji Abdul Basitt (so named because of his pilgrimage to Mecca) still does the same with his family.

Haji Abdul welcomes me into his stone home in Sofi to talk about coffee. I duck inside the cool chamber and leave the arid heat behind me. Haji Abdul chews a steady stream of chat leaves, punctuated by the occasional sip of *hasher*, a brew made from coffee husks.

"We drink hasher more often than we do the coffee leaves," he tells me. "The husks have better flavor." He pours a long stream of butterscotch-colored brew into a tin mug. "The husks are also more addictive," he says.

He smiles, and his gums are green from the chat, soon to be washed clean by the hasher.

Haji Abdul, like others in Sofi, dries his coffee on his home's whitewashed flat roof. Together we go up to survey the beans. They're spread in a single layer under the watchful presence of the rounded stone roof of the neighboring Muslim shrine. Haji Abdul cannot produce as much coffee today as he could fifteen years ago. His production has dropped 80 percent because of the drought. "Will you keep producing coffee?" I ask.

Haji points to the shrine behind us. "It's important," he says. "People come here from all over to worship. During this time, they need coffee. I will stay with coffee because of this ritual."

Haji himself rarely drinks coffee. When he does, it's laden with sugar. Salt flavors the hasher. As we talk, children flow in and out of his compound. I ask Haji how many children he has.

"Children? They do not drink any of the brews until they are old enough to work in the field—fourteen or fifteen, that is when they start."

Soon, we are discussing farming, and it is not until twenty minutes later that I realize he never answered my question. I think of a saying I have heard: that in Ethiopia you count your oxen, count your cows, but never your children. It is bad luck. I wish Haji good luck as we bid each other farewell.

Opposite: **Coffee cherries drying on Haji Abdul Basitt's roof, with the Sofi Shrine in the background.**
Overleaf: **Haji Abdul Basitt climbing to his rooftop.**

RETURNING TO COFFEE

In the heart of the Chercher Mountains, west of Harar, the elders of Hirna have gathered to talk about coffee. Mohammed Abdo Aidir, Sheik Abdullah Abrit, and Ato German Wendafrash cluster with me around a table. We eat roasted barley and popcorn as a woman prepares coffee beside us. Mohammed Abdo Aidir—Ato Mohammed—is from Yemen, but he likes Ethiopia better. He tells me stories of the trading between Ethiopians, Yemenis, Italians, Greeks, and Armenians in the 1960s. They'd trade coffee for fabrics, spices, and more.

Ato Mohammed smiles when he talks of those days. "We all get along," he says. "We go to each other's holidays. Do you know that?"

He is eighty-three years old and wears a pinstripe pink and teal shirt with dress pants and shoes. I tuck my own worn walking shoes under my chair and sit up straighter as we talk. When I ask him about his earliest memory of coffee, he tells me he does not remember ever not having a memory of coffee.

When I ask the elders what they think of chat, they tell me that their community is leaving chat behind. The eastern highlands have recently switched back to planting more coffee, they say. Coffee prices have enabled farmers to maintain their coffee commitment. "You will see," Ato Mohammed says. "Go to Masalaa today and see why coffee is what we are supposed to have. Masalaa is coffee. Coffee. Coffee."

Mohammed Abdo Aidir in Hirna.

FREEDOM TO WORSHIP A STONE

Keela is a Muslim name and Chele a Christian name for a coffee preparation from the eastern mountains that's steeped in mysticism and rites of sacrifice. I speak to a Muslim woman who prepares Keela, but she will only relate details about the making of the dish, deflecting any questions about its meaning. Nor will she tell me her name. When I ask her how old she is, she tells me there are five generations below her.

"Can anyone make this?" I ask.

"Only special people can make it," she tells me. "Only special people can even touch it."

She tells me that the seeds are dried and boiled until they become very dark. Butter is added at a precise point in the boiling and left to cook with the beans throughout. Only when the beans are soft is the pot removed from the stove, after which the mixture is transported to another holy vessel and left to sit overnight. Observants practice Keela/Chele during Timket (January). Animal sacrifices often accompany the thickened, congealed coffee dish; true believers in fact think they will fall ill and disaster befall their families if they don't observe the ritual. This is all the woman will tell me. Later, I ask Mohammed Abdo Aidir about Keela.

"It is a belief like any other," he says. "You can believe in whatever you want. Even those who want to worship a stone are free to do so." The other men surrounding us nod. They are Christian, Muslim, Oromo, Yemeni, Harari—their noncommittal answer doesn't surprise me. This, after all, is the trading crossroads of Africa and the Middle East. Anything goes.

Below: **Elder in Hirna.**
Opposite: **Women outside of a church in Gonder.**

PASTOR MUHAMMAD

"Pastor Muhammad lives in Wollo," Teddy tells me, mentioning a province in northeastern Ethiopia.

I nod while trying to think about why this might matter to me.

"Pastor. Muhammad?" Teddy says.

"Ah," I say. "Only in Ethiopia."

Modern Ethiopia is a collage of various religions and beliefs. Mosques alternate with churches, and bells of both faiths chime separately and in synchronicity. In most of Ethiopia's cities, religious tolerance comes naturally and is part of everyday cultural expression. The ease is born from centuries of side-by-side living. People joke that Ethiopia could be the best destination for vegetarian tourism because every day—somewhere, somehow—someone is fasting, abstaining from meat for religious reasons. So far, the concept has yet to make it into any travel brochures. The aura of mutual religious acceptance, however, is undisputable.

"What do you remember about the biggest difference between Muslims and Christians when you were growing up?" I ask Teddy.

"Who kills the animals for the meat," he says. He explains that Christians will not eat meat slaughtered by a Muslim, and vice versa. Teddy remembers growing up and having two sets of meat for when fasts would be broken, in his house and the houses of friends.

Most adult Ethiopians you talk to today have stories of growing up in relative religious harmony in the larger cities and towns. Tolerance was expected, though easier to extend in some situations. Since the turn of the twenty-first century, that harmony has been put to the test. Ethiopia's geographically central position as the Horn of Africa is a big factor. The elders I met seemed always to shrug when I asked them about people of other faiths. In a country with more than two hundred dialects and endless permutations of socio-cultural allegiance, difference is never distant. How those differences will continue to be tolerated remains to be seen. Most people are hoping that the need for harmony of the many will supersede any desire for singular hegemony. It's no small task given the various groups seeking acknowledgement and a government that, making matters more complex yet, responds differently to different groups. Here in the cradle of humanity, one hopes the longstanding tolerance will not only win out, but spread.

COFFEE'S RELIGIOUS CROSSROADS

Coffee existed in Ethiopia for centuries before it was consumed via an infusion, in the way it's most commonly drank today. By most accounts, coffee was first infused in Arabia; thus when it came back into Ethiopia around 1780 as an infusion, it was predominantly enjoyed by Muslims. The Sufi mystics and the ruling classes used it to stay alert and awake, combining it often with chat.

At this time, Christians were dead set against coffee because of the Muslim association. Coffee then was also being used in spirit possession (Zar) ceremonies, and in Oromo healing ceremonies and blessings. The multifarious threat of coffee to the Christian way of life even created decrees against the drink.

The Ethiopian church's strictures against coffee began to crumble with the urbanization of Addis Ababa. Coffee use was rampant in the Ethiopian countryside at this time—the late 1880s—as it was throughout the world. (Coffee was served in urban coffee houses all the way from Yemen to England, Turkey to France, and Holland to Brazil by this time—and had been, in some cases, for two hundred years.) By the turn of the twentieth century, the Ethiopian church, sensing a losing battle, quickly co-opted coffee for its own uses and soon wove it into one of their most important rituals: Ledata. Ledata is the celebration of Saint Mary and takes place on the first of every month, with the largest ceremony, in Genbot (May/June), regarded as Mary's actual birthday.

The church was so effective in their hijacking of coffee that in just a few decades the use of coffee became automatically associated with Christian ritual. Christians made up roughly 50 percent of the population at this time and were the ruling class. Ironically, the elements of the actual ceremony then as now blend many threads from coffee's history, with the following key components:

• Muslim Influence: *Jebena* is an Arabic word, and the potbellied vessel itself is thought to have originated in Arabia. The primary words to denote the stages of the coffee ceremony are also Arabic. As Rita Pankhurst describes, "*Awol* and *abol* are derived from *awwal*, meaning 'first, old, preceding'; *thani* [also called *tona, tola*, and *hulatana*] is the Arabic for 'second'; and *baraka* comes from the Arabic *baraka*, 'blessing.'"

• Zar Ceremonial Influence: An extra cup often exists for the spirit's enjoyment; the tray, called *rekebot* (trough), is raised on the sides for the spirit's consumption. In many renditions, coffee is poured in a steady stream and moved from cup to cup without breaking the flow, creating a natural overflow into the rekebot. The burning of incense and resins is also rooted in the Zar practice.

• Oromo Influence: The Oromo have long used coffee ceremoniously, with prayers and blessings—for reconciliation, atonement, hope for life following death, healthy livestock, and more. The weight of the modern coffee ceremony is often credited to this influence.

Resting before, and after, Orthodox ceremonies in Gonder.

Overleaf: South in the Chercher Mountains awaits an oasis of abundance twenty-eight kilometers from the busy roadside town of Hirna. We turn toward Masalaa and drive through drizzle to fields as green and evenly grazed as golf courses, with teff, mangos, bananas, and sugarcane leaning into the river. Sorghum fields fill horizons in every direction. This is the Ethiopia of my imagination. Papaya grows across the water. Coffee is omnipresent, while chat is absent. Thick-walled caves stand guard on the hillsides, their daggered stalactites so agleam with water that you can practically hear it drip a mile off.

COFFEE SACRIFICE

Buna Kale is the "slaughtering of the coffee," a term used in the Oromo region for a ceremonial sacrifice (in which coffee replaces an animal in order to change fate). Buna Kale is often used to ward off sickness, to call for rain, to mourn the loss of livestock, and to pray for better times. In Hararge, Buna Mekontet, "pinching of coffee," serves a similar purpose.

Some researchers have called this practice a "coffee slaughter." The removal of the tip of the coffee cherry is likened to the removal of a woman's breast, or a cut into an animal.

COFFEE FROM MOHAMMED

Ahmed Zecharria, a historian at the National Museum in Addis Ababa, tells me a rarely recounted Islamic tale of coffee origin. According to this legend, the Prophet Mohammed's grandchildren, Hassan and Hussein, were one day being bathed by their mother. When she finished the day's bath, coffee beans sprouted from the water. Those beans were then used for prayers, beginning the Muslim use of coffee beans in ceremony, and of the leaves and husks for daily consumption. The story dates back to the middle seventh century.

COFFEE STORY: ETHIOPIA

MORNINGSIDE COFFEE IN HARAR

Mornings are marked by quick coffees in shops and cafés that range from full-service establishments to single wooden tables along the road. In Hararge, try a Chi Buna Spris—a mix of coffee and black tea poured over two heaping spoonfuls of sugar. When the drink arrives at your table, each layer is clearly separated from the others until you blend them with a delicate spoon.

SUN-DRIED REVOLUTION

Naturally processed coffee has swept through Ethiopia like a revolution—or so you might think if you read the coffee news. In reality, Ethiopia has been naturally processing its coffees for centuries. Up until the turn of the twenty-first century, however, natural processing was seen as a cheap, rural method. Truly sophisticated coffee was obtained through industrial means—in this case, the washing process.

Today, Ethiopia produces some of the highest-rated washed and naturally processed coffees in the world. In order to put naturally processed coffees atop the quality ladder, Ethiopia has had to extend her reach right into the cups of small roasters worldwide.

Coffee buying has long been the domain of large import companies. During the late 1980s and '90s, however, individual roasters started to send buyers directly to coffee's sources where possible—at the time, largely Central and South America. When "going to origin" became possible in Ethiopia, after the fall of the Derg in the early 1990s, the roasters quickly formed a strong connection to sun-dried coffees. People wanted more distinct and nuanced coffees, and the appreciation for single-origin coffees—beans sourced and processed in the highly selective manner of each specific region—skyrocketed. The world was ready for coffee to be more than coffee. The Ethiopian sun-dried revolution helped enable this change.

"Nature created sun-dried coffee," Abdelluh Bagersh, the head of a well-established Ethiopian export company, tells me. "Why shouldn't we drink it?"

Bagersh was working with sun-dried coffees during the coffee crisis at the turn of this century. The crisis created global awareness of the coffee business—and of the abominably low wages coffee farmers all too often made. Fair Trade—the standardized system of transparency that attempts to implement a working wage for farmers—in fact had its raison d'être with coffee at this time.

Although the world had been aware of these issues for years preceding the crisis, this crossroads finally created a demand for Fair Trade coffees: people wanted to know where their money was going. This in turn drew more attention to the entire coffee process. Sun-dried coffees were just starting to emerge as something new to appreciate in Ethiopia—something that preserved flavor instead of homogenizing it through a washing process. Today, Fair Trade is just one of commercial coffee's potential qualifiers. Other certifications have arisen to address environmental practices (Organic Certification, Rainforest Alliance Certification) and buying practices (Direct Trade). The certifications present both a benefit and a hurdle for farmers and millers, as each certification demands the farmer or miller have on hand an initial surplus of money to qualify for something he might already be doing, or additional capital to create new practices. The coffee community is still not entirely settled on its ultimate stamp of human-labor and land-use fairness. In the meantime, dedicated participants throughout the coffee chain are working toward a better product. In Ethiopia, many are adding or returning to sun-dried coffees to offer a unique flavor profile from their village or region. Currently, many of the large processing stations in Ethiopia have installed raised beds for sun-dried coffees. The capacity to process coffees in small, distinct batches is highlighted through this processing.

Opposite: **Sun-drying coffee cherries outside Amaro Kele.**

VALUE IN THE MIDDLE

Specialty coffee creates a unique relationship between the coffee farmer and the coffee miller. Each places a high value on quality, and needs his compatriot to do the same for the best potential final product. Coffee farmers pick better cherries; coffee millers process those cherries with specific techniques. Millers, in this way, are like vintners. They take the raw material and through careful processing and extensive attention to drying times, rot pre-vention, and innovation preserve the cherries' true flavor. "Middlemen"—be they millers, buyers, sellers, or other processors—are never revered, and they have a complicated history in the coffee world as the greatest exploiters. The hope is that the move toward a sophisticated understanding of coffee similar to our appreciation of wine will demand more transparency with each step, and in turn allow for the value to be seen throughout the chain.

THE BARISTA AS THE BOTTLE

Baristas create the final flourish on coffee's journey. World barista competitions—where coffee professionals face off against each other in a skills showdown of coffee making and coffee knowledge—have thousands of competitors in dozens of countries and are increasing in numbers annually. Unlike wine, which ships bottled and can be opened virtually anywhere, by any one, to the same effect, a well-produced green coffee requires sophisticated roasting and brewing by, respectively, a roaster and a barista to unlock its value. That is, artful brewing best expresses the essential source.

Opposite: **Drying coffee at a mill in Amaro Kele.**
Below: **Barista in Gonder.**

THE COFFEE RUSH

In Golecha, southwest of Nazeret, a coffee community stands in growing eminence. Previously, all of Golecha's coffee would be exported to Harar, four hundred kilometers away by dilapidated road. New development has created a separate category so that Golecha coffees are now listed as their own coffees instead of as Harar coffees, and the road has undergone dramatic improvements. The result has been an 80 percent increase in the price of the coffee. Farmers who used to plant chat have returned to coffee.

"Farmers are planting as many coffee trees as they can," Muhammed Gunde, a man on the *woreda* (neighborhood) board, says. "We make 70 percent of our income from coffee."

"Has there been a time without coffee in Golecha?" I ask.

"There is always buna!" he says. "We don't even drink Huja [the Golecha name for tea with coffee leaves, milk, and salt] anymore, because there is just so much buna."

"No one drinks Huja?" I ask.

"Only the old people. The young people want coffee." Muhammed slaps his knees emphatically. "For young people, buna is real buna. If a woman wants to marry a man, she has to make the best buna or she will not get married."

"Is it about how the buna tastes?" I ask.

Muhammed shakes his head. "It is about how the woman prepares it," he says.

He is twenty-four, and tells me that there has not yet been a woman who prepares his coffee right. "Soon," he says.

Left: **Family coffee preparation in Kaffa.**
Opposite: **Girl in Sidamo.**

COFFEE'S USES

COFFEE SALVE

Throughout Ethiopia, grounds are used as a paste and an antiseptic on cuts, creating a salve that is re-applied until an injury heals.

KESHIR

Many Oromos in eastern Ethiopia make Keshir, a combination of coffee from the bean and roasted barley in its husk. Garlic and ginger are added for flavor, and sesame for oiliness to make a thicker brew. The brew is used especially for those with respiratory problems.

ASHARA & HOJA

Ashara, the Oromo name for the drink with coffee husks, is most often consumed in the eastern highlands. Harari usually drink *hoja* (the Harari word for the same) with milk in the morning, after chewing chat. Beans are reserved for special occasions, as they are in the city.

KUTI'S ECONOMICS & EXCEPTIONS

The Harari have again and again made the economic decision to drink kuti from coffee's leaves, and save the bean for sale. Exceptions are made for ceremony, including:

▣ After a woman gives birth, she has forty days of seclusion with her new child and family. A coffee ceremony breaks this seclusion, with coffee roasted with butter to signify a new, bountiful life.

▣ Coffee is used to mark circumcision (male and female), readings from the Koran, and to break the thirty-day period of mourning following a death.

Left: Grinding roasted coffee by hand in Hirna.
Opposite: Nuare Roasted Coffee factory in Harar.

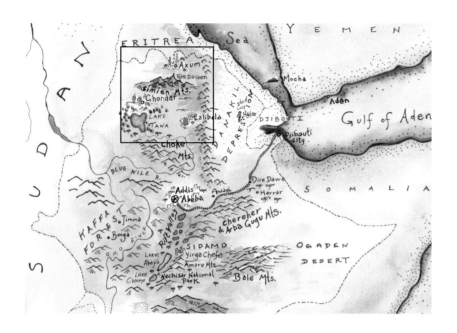

NORTHERN HIGHLANDS

Ethiopia's northern reaches hold its greatest known treasures and most compelling mysteries. On the far border of the Tigray region, the ancient kingdom of Axum is still revealing her power to archeologists today—two thousand years after the height of her rule. Today, Tigray is known as the epicenter of Ethiopia's rock-hewn churches. Many of these religious enclaves date back to the seventh century and are carved into vertical rock faces and/or accessed by near-vertical rocky terrain.

South of Tigray, the Amhara Region encompasses the heart of the Northern Highlands. Amhara holds the Simien Mountains and Ethiopia's tallest point—Ras Dashen (4,543 meters)—as well as Lake Tana, its largest lake. Amhara is also home to Lalibela, Ethiopia's twelfth- and thirteenth-century capital and site of some of its richest historical and architectural heritage in the monolithic and semi-monolithic churches found there.

Traditions and land are equally ancient in these parts of Ethiopia. Coffee serves as a link from all of these elements from the past through today.

ARID PRIDE

It's been raining in Tigray. For three months, the skies have poured water on the arid swath of land that makes up Ethiopia's northern edge. New trees sprout in moist soil beds suspended in rocky terraces; ephemeral lakes reflect a constant possibility of abundance; and endless permutations of green edge their way into the earthen landscape.

It's 2010, and Tigray has had its wettest rainy season in thirty years. The land is drunk with optimism. So drunk that a man named Haile tells me he might even plant coffee.

"We need to," he says, "because Tigrayans drink the most coffee in Ethiopia."

"Did you know people in Sidamo say the same?" I ask him.

Haile laughs. "And in Oromia, Harar . . . all Ethiopians drink the most coffee."

Haile mainly farms barley, and he tells me he's never seen coffee grown in the Gheralta region, where he lives, though he drinks it every day. He tells me there are places in Tigray that still hold on to coffee, but here the land has been too arid for too long for him to grow it. "Maybe now," he says, "if it keeps raining, things will change."

Haile tells me this as we sit in the shade of a four-hundred-meter sandstone face. From our perch, we can see Tigray spiraling beneath us, terraces dancing around clusters of rock towers and pathways lacing between them, linking homes, villages, and towns. This is the land of one of the greatest famines in Ethiopian history—in 1984. That was before Haile was born, but he holds a collective memory of that time.

"In Tigray," he tells me, "we save things. We stretch out our happiness this way. Coffee is first to be saved."

Haile, as well as many other Tigrayans, adds barley to his coffee, parceling out coffee beans judiciously for his family, splurging with 100 percent coffee for guests. When I ask him if there is a moment when he is drinking barley and not coffee, he shakes his head.

"Even one coffee bean makes it buna," he says.

Opposite: **The main Gheralta Massif, Tigray.**
Right: **Fields in Megab.**

COFFEE'S SELFISHNESS

"Do you understand why coffee was banned by the church?" Ghebremedhim Gebru Kidame asks me.

Gebru is the manager at the Gheralta Lodge outside Hawzien, Tigray, and a historian on the side. I've been asking him questions about coffee for days, but this is the first time he has asked me one.

"Can you tell me the story?" I say.

"It was a long time ago," Gebru explains, "back when Jesus died—the time of the great sacrifice. Everything mourned for Jesus then—the rivers were dry, the wind still, and the trees were dry. There were no flowers, seeds, or leaves."

He pauses, checking to see if I am following the story. I nod him along, pen poised midair.

"Except for coffee," Gebru says. "Coffee was the only plant that did not cry for Jesus."

Below: **Gebru Kidame.**
Left: **Abuna Yemata Guh.**

"Imagine," Gebru continues, "coffee green when all of the other trees are sad." He shakes his head.

"For how long?" I ask.

"So long the priests could point to the only green tree in the world and say not to drink it."

Gebru and I have shared coffee twice already. "But you drink it now, right?" I say.

"Just now—for twenty years. Never before then," Gebru says. When he was a child, Genru was told that if he drank coffee he would not make it to paradise. Coffee would keep him from heaven, and the church, in turn, kept him from coffee.

When I ask him why things changed, why people stopped believing in coffee's sin, he tells me that legends only last so long.

"This is a story," he tells me, smiling. "Only a story. You understand that, don't you?"

LAKE TANA

One still moment in the middle of Lake Tana is enough to convince anyone that Ethiopia has the lushest landscape on Earth. Dusky volcanic water roils beneath a yellowed surface that mutes a horizon stippled by hippos, crocodiles, pelicans, and fishermen. Papyrus reeds line the southern shore; thirty-seven islands punctuate the landscape. The great lake, at eighty-four kilometers by sixty-six kilometers and with an average depth of nine meters, is Ethiopia's largest. Lake Tana was formed by volcanic blockage that reversed the flow of the Blue Nile and created Tis Asat—the Blue Nile Falls. The forty-five-meter falls isolated the lake and enabled Tana to develop its own endemic fauna. In 2003, a hydroelectric station was completed that reduced the falls from a constant roar to a mere trickle. The building of the stations was (and still is) a highly contested development.

Long labeled the direct source of the Blue Nile, which in turn is the greatest source, by volume, of the Nile proper, Lake Tana is actually 177 kilometers downstream of the true source, the village of Gish Abay.

From the fourteenth through the seventeenth centuries, Lake Tana was fundamental in preserving Christianity in Ethiopia. During this time, Tana was a safe haven for royal artifacts and the tombs of emperors. Most of the monasteries on the lake were built during this period, many of them atop ancient ruins of even older religious sites. The legacy of all the monasteries, from the various epochs, offers a historical chronicle of Orthodox Christianity in Ethiopia. Tana Qirqos island alone is said to be home to a rock upon which the Virgin Mary rested on her way back from Egypt, as well as the prior home of the Ark of the Covenant, kept at the Tana Qirqos monastery from 400 BC to 400 AD before it was moved north to Axum.

All of Tana's treasures were kept safe within the vast woodlands of Tana's many islands, arrayed in their great maze. Currently, there are more than three dozen churches on the lake, twenty of which grow coffee. According to local legend, coffee, the lake, and Christianity are forever entwined.

COFFEE BY DECREE

In 1307, Abuna (Bishop) Betre Mariam established a settlement on the Zege Peninsula, on the northeast corner of Lake Tana. The inhabitants gathered and asked Abuna Betre Mariam what crops they should live on. As an answer, he broke his prayer stick into three and planted the pieces in the ground.

The next day, three crops had established themselves—coffee, hops, and lemon—and Abuna Betre Mariam made the people promise that they would cultivate only these crops. The decree still holds today, over seven hundred years later.

Menelik Alemu tells me this story. He is a thirty-year-old farmer who's spent the past two years working on exporting Zege's coffee to the world. "We made a promise to God," he says. "It is ours to keep."

Ten thousand people now depend on Zege's crops, of which coffee comprises 80 percent of the agricultural activity. When Menelik tells me this, my eyes widen in surprise.

"We believe that the first coffee plant in Ethiopia was found here in Zege," he says.

Anticipating my next question, he continues, "When Christianity came from Axum and reached Tana, coffee began spreading here."

As I take notes, I look up in time to catch him standing.

"There is a book about this," he says.

I wonder if he is going to get the book, but he sits back down. "I think it is also written as such in German," he says, sighing. "But we all know that coffee comes from Kaffa, so this can't be right."

We're quiet for a moment. Pelicans croak in the distance. Wood chatters as children build piles for the following week's transport across the lake. A young girl runs up and stops quickly when she sees me. Menelik waves at her. She comes closer.

"It's good to still keep our promise," he says.

Left: **Boy outside his home on the Zege Peninsula.**
Opposite: **A sunrise paddle to market, Lake Tana.**

EPHEMERAL WATERWAYS

Lake Tana's papyrus boats, *tankwa*, have an ephemeral life. They are constructed by the Waito tribe from tightly bound bundles of thick grass and turned over to face the sun for daily drying. Still, their average life span is only three to four weeks. On Fridays, the lake is full of boats transporting wood from Zege to Bahir Dar. It's a seven-hour paddle in each direction, but worth it for both the farmers (for the money) and the buyers (for the dense, high-quality wood). At any given moment on a Friday, you can gaze out upon countless boats in mid-journey to, or returning from, Bahir Dar. The boats carry other necessary goods during the rest of the week, transporting oxen, food, and people across the vast lake.

Today, we are on the water from sunrise to sunset. At the end of the day, we see a lone boatman paddling up from Lake Tana's mouth and Nile outlet. His boat is barely above water; fresh papyrus reeds load down his bow. He straddles the boat, with water coming up to his mid-thigh. He has an hour to paddle to shore. When we ask if he thinks he will make it in time to build his next boat, he tells us he always does.

ZEGE'S LUCK

The Zegenia people believe in coffee for luck. Most of the luck they seek has to do with the market and how their trading will fare. Normally, Zegenians drink coffee three times a day, imbibing three cups each time. If someone is in a hurry, however, he'll often stop and grab a bean to crush in his teeth for protection. Better this than to skip coffee altogether.

Abol, the first cup of coffee, is the most important one not to miss. If a visitor arrives after Abol has been drunk, most families will offer to add more coffee powder to the jebena so the visitor can also have abol coffee and the luck that comes with it. Women traditionally make the coffee, and there are many stories of men blaming their bad luck at market on the timing or quality of their morning coffee. It's mostly men who tell those stories.

Many in Zege further believe their luck will be the best if the coffee they drink is prepared in their home in the morning. This will extend the blessing to their entire house.

Brothers in the shade of an enset tree, Zege Peninsula.

DEVOTION VIA COFFEE

Zege coffee traditions are steeped in the Christian expression of the coffee ceremony in Ethiopia. All of the traditional practices—those that incorporate the Arabic names, Muslim offerings, and Zar and Oromo elements—are expressed each time coffee is consumed. The one exception is on Sabbath. Roasting and grinding coffee the moment before you boil it is customary. However, the provisions of the true Sabbath dictate no tool use on that day. In Zege, people prepare for Sabbath by roasting and grinding the coffee the day before, or, in the case of knowing a less observant neighbor, finding someone else to do the work on the holy day.

Priest inside Ura Kidane Mihiret, Zege Peninsula.

ONE MACHINE, TEN THOUSAND PEOPLE

Menelik invites me to his house. "I will show you how we process our coffee," he says. "Follow me."

The footpaths through the peninsula are worn, bending sharply. This is forest coffee territory, where birds determine the arboreal array by how they eat and void the seeds. Menelik lopes easily through the corridors, crossing trails, skipping obvious intersections, and winding us always deeper into the island. The coffee trees surrounding us are six meters tall. They hide his concrete house until we come upon it.

Menelik's house is locked. No one knew we were coming. He yells for a neighbor to come over and let us in. The yells echo off and then die within the dense canopy, not carrying all the way to the water. "He must be at the lake," Menelik says. He yells more loudly.

Sheep lounge in the shade, plump and drowsy. Menelik says they get fat on coffee here. They eat the pulp from his machine. He adds that he has never seen a goat eat anything from a coffee seed, even though he knows the Khaldi legend by heart.

After a while, we get a key and enter the three-room house. Someone has plastered magazine pages to almost every wall. There is a bed, sometimes two, in each room. Menelik goes to the far room and swoops up the bed coverings, and I spot a flash of red metal underneath.

It takes three people to pull out his pulping machine. It's a disc pulper—they pour water into it and turn it by hand. Menelik's mother had to get a license to run the machine. However, he tells me, she has never used it. "It's mine," he says. This machine, and Menelik's perseverance, has helped create a name for Zege coffee—and a level of appreciation for it as a unique coffee from Ethiopia's Northern Highlands. According to the peninsula residents, it was only a matter of time before the rest of the world came to understand what the Zegenians have always known.

Opposite: **Lake Tana.**
Right: **Menelik with his pulper, on the Zege Penninsula.**

ENTOS EYESU MONASTERY

Entos Eyesu was built in the fourteenth century. One of the few monasteries for women on Lake Tana, it was a refuge until it became a prison in the mid-1800s. When it was re-opened as a monastery, men joined women as residents. Aba Gebre Mechan is the father here, and when I ask him why they now have men, he tells me that they needed men to perform mass.

Aba Gebre adds that he does not know what they did before. "That was not my time," he tells me before he ducks into yet another round stone building, preserved as a cell now for visitors. "But this," he continues, "is where the people were kept."

Coffee is a prime earner also for Lake Tana's monasteries. Here, the monks pick it, dry it, and hull it with a *meg:* a two-piece volcanic-rock system purchased from the Waito tribe (who also make the papyrus boats), at the southern outlet of the great lake. While many of the monasteries grow coffee on Lake Tana, none of the monks are allowed to drink it. They use it to provide income, and sell it primarily in Bahir Dar.

Aba Gebre Mechan.

COFFEE STORY: ETHIOPIA

DRINK COFFEE, KILL HUNGER

Amsaya Anteneh grew up in Bahir Dar; he now lives in Addis and researches coffee yields for his PhD. "Do you know about coffee and hunger?" he asks me.

"Coffee kills the hunger," he says. "Or that's at least what we say. We are a country always with famine, where coffee replaces food."

"The country with the most famine drinks the most coffee?" I ask. It seems wrong even to say it.

"At least this is how we try and trick ourselves," Amsaya says. "Even in my family, in Bahir Dar where we had food during the great famine, we drank it three times a day and people considered it as food."

We talk about this as we sit on the third floor of a mall in central Addis, sipping coffee. "Coffee makes me hungry," I say to Amsaya.

He laughs. "Then you are not Ethiopian."

BREWING LEAVES

In times of drought, coffee leaves are used instead of berries. In Zege, the leaves are brewed with salt, ginger, and fenugreek. Fenugreek itself is often prescribed for diabetics or those with colds. Buna Shai is the name for the tea, but most people I meet make a face when I mention it. "Buna is better," they say.

Gonder market.

BETA ISRAEL

The Beta Israel is a name for a group of Ethiopian Jewish communities who historically surrounded Lake Tana and Gonder in the Northern Highlands. Beta Israel are commonly associated with the lost Israelite tribe of Dan, though other stories place them as descendents of King Solomon and the Queen of Sheba, or potential descendents of Ethiopian Christians who converted to Judaism. The Beta Israel, called by the derogatory name "Falasha" in the ancient Ethiopian tongue Ge'ez, were said to number more than half a million in the 1500s, when the group had autonomy in worship, government, and family structure.

Autonomy collapsed in the early 1600s, when the practice of the Jewish religion was forbidden. While many Beta Israel were either killed or forced into slavery and/or religious conversion, many of the Jewish practices survived in the centuries to follow. During the Derg, under the Ethiopian rule of Mengistu Haile Mariam, the Beta Israel faced severe persecution—so much so that

a rescue effort was launched by Israel. From 1977 to 1991, more than thirty thousand Beta Israel were relocated to Israel. The most concentrated effort, called Operation Solomon, took place in May 1991, when during a thirty-six-hour period more than fourteen thousand people were airlifted across the Red Sea.

Currently, there are an estimated one hundred twenty thousand Beta Israel, with the majority residing in Israel. They are now almost entirely absent from Ethiopia. Alongside the Beta Israel are the Falash Mura, defined as a people with either Jewish ancestry or who were previously Jews themselves and were forced to convert to Christianity. Today's Falash Mura on Ethiopian soil number between three thousand and six thousand, with many seeking to emigrate to Israel. Behind the numbers lies a belief held by Ethiopian Jews, religious scholars, and historians that the ancient land of Abyssinia has always had Judaism at her core and running throughout her legends.

COFFEE IN HIDING

While coffee was for sale at market in Gonder and Axum in the early 1800s, the Ethiopian Orthodox Church remained strongly opposed to the drink. The beans were traded to Muslims, called "Mohammedans" at that time in Ethiopia, and any consumption was frowned upon because of the Muslim involvement.

Ironically, Zar spirit-possession rituals involving coffee were also then taking place. The northern Ethiopian highlands are thought to be the home of Zar, and those who practiced it were of differing faiths—Christian, Muslim,

Beta Israel. Christians made up the majority, and the rituals often blended the faiths to rid possessed persons of their Zar spirits. It was not until a hundred years later that coffee was openly consumed by those of all faiths in the streets of Gonder. Today, every doorway you look through has a jebena either in use or waiting to brew the next round of buna.

Left: **Wheat field in Gonder.**
Below: **Market-bound outside Gonder.**

BEANS FOR BULLETS & BEYOND

A common statistic you'll hear in Ethiopia is that only 50 percent of the coffee is actually exported. By most accounts, this is true. The reasons for this, however, vary. Local consumption is exceedingly high, and in some of the remotest areas in Ethiopia this can drop exports to less than 5 percent. Inside the trading hubs of the country, however, black-market sales greatly contribute to the "leakage." During the Derg's reign, a familiar saying was that every coffee bean grown represented a bullet for Ethiopia. Today, while the government takes much less oppressive punitive measures against its citizens, the sentiment that each coffee bean represents more than a bean—in fact, means economic independence—is still present. Sudan, Somalia, and Djibouti are the primary recipients of the black-market beans. This trading theatre garners a 10 percent margin compared to the standard 3 percent margin in sanctioned trading. Many coffee exporters in Ethiopia see the valuation of specialty coffee as a means to combat the leakage, given the available loftier price point for higher-quality coffees. Everyone agrees that the leakage needs to be addressed for Ethiopia to fully actualize its coffee potential.

COFFEE'S DEEPEST ROOTS

Three thousand years ago, the Queen of Sheba ruled Ethiopia. Known in Abyssinia as Makeda, she ruled during the tenth century BC. Her story is among the most important in Ethiopia, as it is her imperial bloodline that created a lasting succession of rulers all the way to the end of Haile Selassie's rule, in 1974. The Queen of Sheba joined with King Solomon in Jerusalem to create this lineage. Although no religious or scholarly accounts directly link the Queen of Sheba to coffee, mentions of coffee during her rule and her use—and even encouragement—of coffee are often mentioned as proof of coffee's enduring legacy in Ethiopia.

Left: **Guard outside Amaro Kele.**
Below: **Family in Gonder.**

ADDIS ABABA

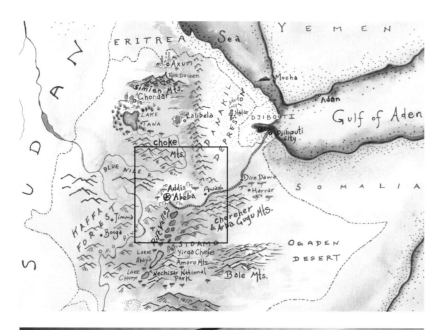

Opposite left: **Dancing.**
Opposite right: **Traditional coffee ceremony.**
Above: **Coffee Shop in Addis Ababa.**
Overleaf: **Runners in Meskal Square.**

Life in Addis Ababa, the center of Ethiopia, is fast paced and slow steeped at the same time. Every facet of Ethiopian life exists in both urban and rural formulation within the city's borders. Addis is Ethiopia's crossroads.

NATIONAL FOOD

"You know what would be the worst for Ethiopia?" Teddy asks me one day as we wend slowly through a head of cattle. "Vegetarianism. We need to eat meat to keep the roads safe."

As if on cue, a young calf speeds into the road. Tires squeal. Teddy smiles. "I eat meat three times a day," he says. "I'm just doing my part."

Cattle are big business in Ethiopia. They're also prized sources of food for much of the country. Many Ethiopian cows have a large cervicothoracic hump that sways independently of their body when they move. Called *shagna* and considered a delicacy, the hump is a dense fat-storage mechanism that allows the cows to withstand lean agricultural conditions. Shagna can be found at butcher shops alongside quartered cows. Meat is often eaten rare, and deworming conversations are common. For those who indulge in cooked meat, it's just as easy to pick your cut at the restaurant. You'll have it in hand moments later, lightly fried and spiced with a touch of *burburri*, ready to be rolled up in your enjera.

Ethiopia's many bounties.

THE RIFT VALLEY

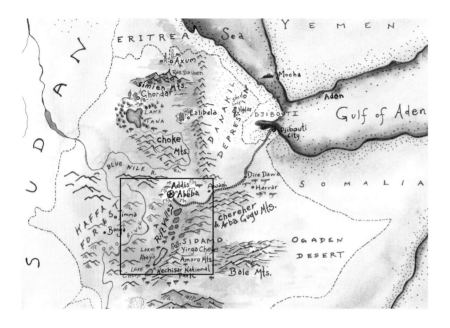

Cities lose their grip quickly in Ethiopia. The concentrated urban center abruptly becomes farmland whichever direction you travel, from whichever city. If you leave Addis Ababa and head south, your new horizon is the Great Rift Valley (aka the Rift Valley). The massive basin stretches, echoingly, fifty-six hundred kilometers diagonally from Syria to Mozambique, straight through the heart of Ethiopia. A three-/two-lane road travels along the center of the Rift Valley—it's three when you need to pass another car, donkey cart, or cattle train, but two the rest of the time. Soon, fields unfold to either side and the city disappears entirely.

Today, the donkeys pull flat carts of teff, a grain integral to Ethiopian life both for its nutritional value and for making enjera. Farmers methodically set sickle to teff, reaping it from the fields. Each handful is deliberately thrown to one side as the farmer alternates between two rows of teff. Soon these handfuls are collected and stacked together. To the untrained eye, the piles look

Rift Valley sunrise.

haphazard; but as they grow, the grain and grass interlace as lattice-work mooring against wind and rain.

I am not a farmer, but when I drive through Ethiopia all I want to do is be one. Cattle march in circles over domesticated grains to release the seeds. Acacia trees offer rare shade under outstretched limbs. In the distance, ancient volcanic uplifts rest quietly, flat-topped and covered in grass. Soon the lakes themselves appear, first as watery horizons punctuated by people washing and farming, and then as full bodies of water that take up the entire eastern view. Lakes Ziway, Langano, Abiyata, Shala, and Awasa dot the bottom of the Rift Valley with periwinkle waters turned yellow in the day's heat. The earth beneath the lakes is constantly churning and pushing against the surface. One day, if scientists are correct, Africa will split in two along this sunken spine.

119

RIFT FERTILITY

Before you even glimpse the bean, the landscape lets you know you're in coffee's embrace. The air gets lighter and suggests a recent rain, or one about to come. Soft limestone crumbles above a river, giving way to hard, blocky basalt that pierces the water's edge. The trees thicken. A red cherry catches the light in the distance. This is where Ethiopian coffee sings most loudly, in today's new symphony of celebrated flavor: from jasmine to rose, lemon to grapefruit, lingonberry to strawberry, cashew to walnut, black pepper to ginger, and countless other cup attributes, each new well-processed coffee from Ethiopia exhibits nuances to fascinate the senses.

SOUTHERN BREADBASKET

Two paved roads split the Rift Valley, bracketing its edges. The eastern edge of the Rift lakes is the southern heart of Ethiopian coffee country; the western edge is the nation's breadbasket and the gateway to the Lower Omo Valley. This western track eventually traces the shorelines of Lake Abaya and Lake Chamo—the Rift Valley's largest lakes. Abaya's sanguine waves lap at golden shores and seem an optical illusion, even when you run your hands through the rusted water. Chamo's traditional blue sparkles more clearly in contrast to Abaya's earthen hues. Both lakes provide fishing resources, wildlife sanctuaries, and tourism to the surrounding valley. They meet at the city of Arba Minch, the nexus of the Eastern Rift's coffee trade. Pockets of coffee cultivation exist in every shaded mountain valley in sight, but the land best suited for coffee lies west. To get there, one must first traverse Nechisar National Park's empty plains into the Amaro Mountains.

Left: **Sidamo home at dawn.**
Below: **Lake Chamo at sunset.**

COFFEE'S REACH

Four hundred kilometers south of Arba Minch, on Ethiopia's southern edge in the Lower Omo Valley, the Dassanech people, formerly called the Gebeb, import trucks filled with coffee husks. The only other food source they import is Kenyan beets, which they use for body decoration. The brew they make from the tea has been a Dassanech staple for generations, though by most accounts, coffee as an endemic crop has not been present in the Lower Omo Valley for centuries. The reach of the husks, and their stability as a crop—in that the husks are dried and hulled, and not subject to fermentation if improperly stored—suggests a longtime trade relationship moving coffee southward from the Ethiopian highlands.

Scenes from Lake Chamo.

COFFEE NOMADS

A Guji man wants to talk about coffee. We stand outside a square, earthen home, he and I and eight others occupying the one sliver of shade beneath the eaves. The land here is not what I am accustomed to for coffee. It is dry—seemingly everywhere. Before the man tells me about the coffee, I say that I want to know where the coffee actually is.

We walk away from the group into the heat of the sun. It is more than 38 degrees Celsius, but I am the only one sweating. We walk up a slight hill. He points into the distance. I look. I see only the same brown dryness. The man lifts his chin and raises his eyes. I do the same, but it is only when I stand on my toes that I see green.

Just out of sight, coffee grows in clusters in the lowlands. The air is lighter here, not thick in the way I automatically associate with coffee forest. When I tell the man this, he tells me forests are different for the Guji.

They plant only during the rainy season, and tend to the coffee judiciously with the scarce water resources. Coffee is consumed daily as a brew, and the Guji also practice *kelo*. In kelo, beans are roasted in butter until they reach their height of potency. Once the beans cool, people place one or two dozen in their mouths, tucking the softened beans between the cheeks and gums to allow a constant flow of caffeine.

"This way," the man says, "we can spend the day without the need to eat. It is like the people who chew chat, but with a coffee bean."

We walk back to the sliver of shade and join the others. I ask who has kelo in their mouths right now.

All of the men say they do. "And you?" I ask a woman.

All of the women shake their heads in response. The man who has been telling me stories and answering my questions—and who still will not give me his name—explains that women don't hold on to the kelo, but have a small amount in the morning and spit it out. Children are not given kelo—it is too strong for them—but they can have as much coffee as they'd like.

The Guji are an ethnic subgroup of the Oromo people and live throughout southern Ethiopia. They are pastoral, if not at times nomadic. When coffee-harvest season arrives, they settle into their temporary homes to pick the cherries, selling everything they can beyond a small stipend for personal use.

"Kelo is smart," the man says. "It uses less coffee. We sell more this way."

"Is there enough coffee here for you?" I ask him.

He looks around as if trying to imagine his home from my eyes. "There is plenty," he says.

Opposite: **Guji group on the outskirts of Nechisar National Park. These men tell me that the Guji tribespeople in the north believe that coffee came directly from the "High Priest From Heaven." The common practice of scattering grain during a coffee ceremony has as its predecessor the same tradition practiced by the Guji and other Oromos. This offering is seen as a direct link to the practice of offering grain in all four directions following the slaughter of an animal. The modern-day understanding of coffee as a blessing ties into this offering from the Oromo.**

EMPEROR SELASSIE'S COFFEE

Today, we are chasing the emperor. We are on the other side of the Amaro Mountains, in the coffee heartland of Sidamo. "Did you know the Emperor Haile Selassie himself drank coffee on our land?" a man asks me over the phone. "High up—on the hill. You should visit."

We make our way off the paved road and switchback up a dirt track on the hillside. Immediately, we drive more slowly as we merge with the foot traffic off the main thoroughfare. People walk in pairs; they rest in the shade. We stop to ask where to go. "Do you know where Haile Selassie drank coffee?" we ask. "We heard it was here."

The responses are all the same: First, a questioning look. Then, a wave to go up higher. An answer—the exact place?

Wouldn't everyone know if the emperor drank coffee here? Wouldn't it be fact? Haile Selassie, king of kings, who ruled an empire through times of greatness, as well as despair—he liked coffee. That is all we know for sure by the end of the road. There is nothing there to mark a visit from Selassie, but nothing to say he didn't visit either.

Opposite top: The Guji's nomadic lifestyle creates a special appreciation for community. Elaborate greetings with great affection are common.
Opposite bottom: The necklace on this young girl signals her virginity, though she does not tell me this. I tell her I like her necklace, and she smiles. It is her older brother who tells me what it means.
Right: Evening in the Rift Valley.

SIDAMO CUPS OF PLENTY

In the highest reaches of southern Ethiopia's Sidamo region, coffee grew wild until the reign of Emperor Menelik II, at the end of the nineteenth century. Today, Sidamo's gentle hills overlay each other with alternating hues of green, and the growing season lasts all year. Well-worn dirt paths follow and intersect rivers and streams. Kelly-green *kulkual* cacti along the trails reach up to ten meters in height. And every grass-thatched home is abutted by the ever forking branches of the coffee trees, with their burgundy cherries.

During Menelik II's time, locals picked coffee by cutting down an entire coffee tree, carrying it to their home, and waiting for the tree to dry and the cherries to simply fall off. They'd then discard the rest of the tree, and use and sell the coffee.

Ato Sha'le Bokal tells us this story. He's the elder in this community of several hundred, the man to whom others come when a dispute needs settling. Born in 1925, he tells me that they now leave the trees in place when they harvest the coffee.

His grandparents told him the story of the trees, as well as other tales. "In those days," he says, "even still when I was a boy, we did not have any cups."

He pauses, as if to confirm that I'm still listening. I nod.

"Do you want to know how they drank the coffee?" he asks.

After I nod again, he says, "They drank it with their hands."

The gathered crowd smiles even before the translator finishes relaying Ato Sha'le's words to me. When Ato Sha'le joins in, his smile erases the eighty-four years on his face.

"No," Ato Sha'le says. "That is not true. Wait, and I will show you the truth."

We're clustered atop evenly grazed grass in the shade of a Dagucho tree. Ato Sha'le asks one of his seventeen children to fetch leaves from a false banana tree—a Woficho. His son returns clutching in one hand a dried leaf and in the other a fresh leaf, and Ato Sha'le selects the dried one first. Ato Sha'le quickly bends and buckles the leaf parchment, stringing a small twig through either end to maintain a bevel deep enough to hold a liquid. Next, he picks up the fresh leaf and through a series of folds reduces the meter-square foliage into a ladle.

Opposite: **Ato Sha'le.**

"A hundred years ago," he says, "this is how we drank coffee." He shows me how they would pass the leaf and share this collective cup.

The dry-leaf vessel easily holds ten times as much coffee as today's omnipresent six-ounce ceramic cups, the kind found in all Ethiopian homes, both urban and rural. I want to ask if coffee seemed more abundant back then—not only on the land, but in the giant cup. Instead, I look around. Coffee trees fill almost the entire backdrop to the horizon, some forty kilometers away. As Ato Sha'le told me earlier, for decades here in Sidamo they'd never done anything with the meaty, red husk of the coffee bean. Other tribes roast the husk and drink the brew. When I asked about this, Ato Sha'le said simply, "It is a sign of plenty when you can throw something away."

We bid goodbye to Ato Sha'le, and then walk an hour back to the road alongside the long afternoon shadows of the coffee trees, deep in the land of plenty that is Sidamo.

ATO SHA'LE'S MACHETE

When I meet Ato Sha'le, it is his machete I notice first. The ornate, silver-wrapped handle is meticulously patterned. After we talk for a few hours, I ask to see it. I hold the machete carefully. "This silver is beautiful," I say.

"That?" he asks. "That is from a battery cover."

I look closer. I can see a faint stamping of familiar letters, though I cannot make out a word.

"Remember," Ato Sha'le says, "we lost everything once, twice, many times. I will show you more." He leaves and comes back dressed in a velour cape with short cotton pants. "This should have been my father's costume," he says. "But the Italians took it all, so I have made it up."

He turns to show me the back of his cape, where a lion decal is glued onto the velour. "This is my costume now," he says.

SIDAMO PROMINENCE

Sidama people currently make up more than 3.5 percent of the Ethiopian population—a testament to the province's mammoth size prior to being officially divided into the Southern People's Region and Oromia during the 1995 repartitioning of Ethiopia. Sidamo's highland position, consistent rainfall, and proximity to the major thoroughfares for centuries maintained its role as an integral contributor to Ethiopia's revenue. Today, the multiple ethnicities in Sidamo intermarry, intercommunicate—with at times as many as eight languages in as many kilometers—and cross-trade, thus layering the difference into a collective whole.

But in the heart of the high country, Sidamo is simply Sidamo. Here, enclosed by dense woods full of hyenas, Columbus monkeys, mangos, guava, and coffee, the Sidama people subscribe to their own traditions. Sidama celebrate their own New Year (Fiche Chembelala) and write in a Latin script. The New Year is a source of pride; the language is a sore spot.

According to legend, a cow ate the old Sidama letters to protect them during times of strife in southern Ethiopia. When the Tigrayan People's Liberation Front (TPLF) took over the government after the Derg, in the 1990s, they slaughtered cattle to feed their troops. The cow that held the letters fell to the knives, and as it was cut apart the letters that tumbled from its belly were all in Latin script. The TPLF forced the Sidama to use these letters, and thus Latin letters are pronounced as if they were Amharic. The Sidama say they have never been able to get their letters back, now that the cow is gone.

A HULLING DANCE

Outside a rectangular mud-and-mortar Sidamo home, a girl, barefoot, sashays a worn limestone rock over drying coffee cherries.

She won't tell me her name, not even as she laughs when I ask for a turn on the rock. Its yellow-gray stone is still warm from her feet, and I place mine exactly as she has, toes curled over the edge. I try to move; the rock stays put. Three women watch from the house nearby, looking worried. I push down harder, crouching to make the rock come to life. The women and the girl stand up taller. They hold their hands palm up and make a lifting motion.

They want me to be lighter.

I'm crushing the cherries.

It's a nine-square-meter patch of recently harvested coffee. Eventually, I spin and swoosh my way in one direction across its length. None of us want me to try returning the other way. Everyone is laughing when the girl retakes her place atop the stone. This rock, which was an unwieldy anchor for me, glides and arcs easily beneath her gentle movements.

COFFEE STORY: ETHIOPIA

COFFEE FOR FLESH & BLOOD

A to Yumatoma has faraway eyes that never meet mine. He sits with his back against a tree in the shade. He tells me he is eighty when we first start talking. Soon thereafter, he tells me he is ninety-two.

"Coffee was created for medicinal purposes," he says. "They used to drink it as a medicine for the flesh and blood."

He picks up a coffee berry and a leaf to show me. He shakes the leaf: "This is for medicine. We wash the blood. Asthma, all of it. Hoja is the name."

"The bean has vitamins. The leaf is better for you," Ato Yumatoma says, "but does not taste as good." He explains how the Sidama take the leaves when they are yellow, and dry them in the sun, roast them, and pound them. "Lightly," Ato Yumatoma says, bringing his hands together gently to show me. Then they boil the powdered leaves in a wide-mouthed pot and add milk.

I ask Ato Yumatoma about using the beans in butter. I want to know if the Sidama do this differently. He shakes his head when I ask him.

"It is very good medicine," he says. His blinks his eyes, and they stick together for a half a beat. They are milky when he opens them. "But today we cannot have it; we don't have butter," he adds.

One of his wives places a hand on his knee. "He is wrong. He was rich," she says. "He always had butter." Ato Yumatoma rests his head against the tree and closes his eyes. He says something, and I lean closer.

"He is only talking to himself now," his wife says. "He is just spinning stories."

"That is what I am here for," I say.

Opposite: Hulling coffee in Sidamo.
Right: Ato Yumatoma.

FARANGE COW

I take a photo of Ato Yumatoma's family. Soon, even before the first Polaroid has developed, his wife is reaching for my arm. She asks me to wait for her—for only a moment.

She disappears into her hut, dipping down automatically to navigate the threshold. I stand near the door, moving closer to feel the cool, welcoming air radiating from the earthen home. I'm trying to look inside without appearing to do so. I tilt my head to get a better vantage point. My eyes meet a cow.

I move out of the way quickly as woman and cow emerge from the hut. The two of them step into the field, turn to face me, and wait.

"Photo?" the woman asks in English.

I pull up the Polaroid camera. I gesture to the rest of her family, behind me. She shakes her head quickly, decisively.

I hold up the camera; the cow looks away. The woman gives the cow's horns a hard tug. They stand together for a moment, and then the cow turns abruptly and trots away.

"Farange!" The woman yells.

I put down the camera. I think she is talking to me. This is what foreigners are often called in Ethiopia.

"Farange!" she says again. I notice she is looking at her cow, not at me.

"Farange?" I ask, pointing at the cow.

The woman nods and tells me, through the translator, that this is what everyone calls their big cows here. She catches the cow and shakes its head. I think it must be the cow's first portrait shoot.

Once the photo cranks out of the camera, the woman heads back inside her home. She tells me that she is getting another cow. I wonder how many more there could be.

AGELESS SIDAMO

"Our grandfathers used to eat honey, milk, and butter, and they lived for one hundred years," a man of sixty tells me. I can barely keep up with him, though I am barely more than half his age. We are hiking quickly together to get home before dusk. The hyenas have been attacking more lately—no one wants to be caught near their den under the cloak of darkness.

"Now we don't have these things, so we die young," the man tells me. He suddenly stops in front of me and I stumble into him. He sighs. I hear a hyena call, close. "I would love [coffee] with butter all the time," he says. And with that he's back to racing down the footpath.

Following page far left: **Coffee cup, Addis Ababa.**
Following page left: **Children in Sidamo.**
Following page right: **Father and daughter in Amaro.**

Below: **A scene from Sidamo.**

CEREMONY THROUGH REPETITION

"Why three cups of coffee?" I ask. Every day. To everyone I meet. I ask everyone this. Most people tell me it is because that is how they have always done it. Here in Sidamo, I get a different answer: "Practice."

Imagine not knowing how to make something—how would you learn? Practice. I'm told people had to experiment to make coffee, causing them to try it in their own homes, starting the tradition of going to other homes to have coffee. Each version would be attempted and sampled, creating a gathering, creating the repetition.

CHILD'S PLAY

In Sidamo, each round of coffee belongs to a different stage of life. Children are prohibited coffee until age five or six, at which point they only get a cup from the diluted third round. Even then, Ato Sha'le says, "they roll around with happiness." The practice of consuming coffee beans steeped in butter is kept for adults. If given beans to hold in their mouths and suck on for the caffeine, the children do not turn out, I am told, as good children.

A pour from the second round comes with puberty. The first round is not shared until a person reaches age twenty-two.

Ato Sha'le's son tells me this. He is just now twenty-three.

"You can get married before you can have the first cup of coffee?" I ask.

"When did I say I could get married?" he laughs. "We can't get married until we are over twenty-two either." I tell him of meeting other families in Ethiopia started by fifteen- and sixteen-year-olds. He tells me that it is not the same in Sidamo. "Age," he says, "governs every choice here."

Social structure and order are evident in the consumption of coffee. Elders are served first, slowly, and the coffee is poured for each member of a family or gathering from oldest to youngest, precisely to demonstrate the honor of age.

CHAT'S LOOSING WAR

Enset, maize, cattle, and wood have all worked in tandem with the coffee crop to sustain Sidamo's economy. The move to chat has not happened here, in part because of its disastrous effect on the soil. Djibouti, chat's main export portal, is far from Sidamo. To give Sidamo's fertile soil over to chat would be at the expense of all the other crops. The payoff, financially, does not make sense. Most farmers I meet in Sidamo are hoping it keeps not making sense.

YIRGA CHEFFE

Yirga Cheffe (also called Yirgacheffe or Yirgachefe) is Ethiopia's best-known coffee region, named for a small town at its center. If you are not paying attention, you can pass the town without even knowing you were there. The larger city of Dila has stretched toward Yirga Cheffe, with a constant stream of people going to the university, markets, and work in Dila. Yirga Cheffe itself was created as a distinct growing region in the 1960s, when its coffees started to gain attention on the world stage—they were singled out for their unique-ness. Later, after political upheaval in the 1970s and '80s, the world attention again returned to Yirga Cheffe.

Yirga Cheffe means "settled marshland" in Amharic. While marshland might not automatically connote beauty, the name belies a fertile center— prime coffee country. Yirga Cheffe's uniqueness has led the way for the current valuation of distinct Ethiopian coffee.

COFFEE SAVORY OR SWEET

Modern Ethiopia is full of coffee cups swirling with sugar. But it wasn't always this way. Salt was the additive of choice until the 1950s, when sugar plantations arrived. Before then, honey had been the primary sweetener available in Ethiopia, though it was reserved for Tej, a fermented beverage popular enough to disallow any surplus honey.

Salt is a primary historic currency in Ethiopia. Today, it is still cut by hand out of the mines in the Danakil Depression—one of Earth's lowest points (155 meters below sea level) and one of its most inhospitable places, with temperatures spiking at 48 degrees Celsius, dust storms, and active volcanoes. Camel trains with Afar herders transport the chalky white and amber blocks hundreds of kilometers, as they have since before the sixth century. The blocks, textbook sized when carried on the camels, are broken down again and again in trade, and finally end up as crystals in your coffee if you choose to drink it the traditional way.

HOLIDAY

"Do you want to know an encouraging story about coffee here?" the academic Rita Pankhurst asks me during an afternoon chat in her garden gazebo back in Addis Ababa.

"Of course," I say.

"There was a group of French agronomists working in Yirga Cheffe," she tells me, "and the man who was involved with the coffee side of their work went back a year later and enquired after a farming friend he had met. He was told his friend was not there. 'Why not?' the agronomist asked, concerned. 'He's on holiday,' they told him.

"'Holiday?' the man asked.

"'He went to Bahir Dar,'" Rita says, ending her story. "Imagine. 'Holiday.' It's absolutely wonderful."

Left & opposite: **Scenes from the start of the day.**

AMARO

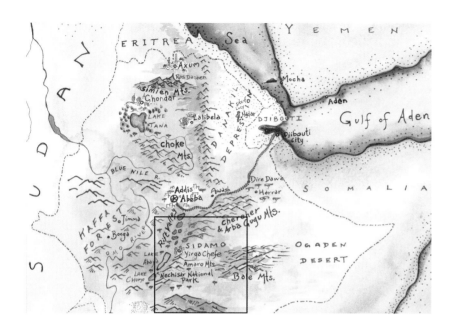

The road into Amaro Kele is not well marked, but that means little in Ethiopia. Thick trees cloak the road we follow out of Yirga Cheffe. We gain altitude into the highland country. We could keep driving this thoroughfare and dip down into Kenya, but instead we tuck west, to Amaro.

The Amaro Mountains cover a sixty-kilometer stretch of highlands that crest at Mount Delo's 3,240-meter summit. Nechisar National Park engulfs much of western Amaro, starting at Lake Chamo and moving to riparian forests, high savannah, and finally to thicketed acacia woodlands.

Today we are on the eastern edge of this land. A dirt road drops into a wide valley stretching twenty-five kilometers until it gives way to the Amaro Mountains on its western edge. We travel the one way into—and out of—Amaro over the course of several hours. Later, I will learn that the land becomes Amaro at the third bridge, just after the shola tree with a trunk as wide as the base of the mud homes in its shadow. This marks your entry into Brigadoon.

CALL ME BONNIE

Woizero Asnakech Thomas has several names. She asks me, at first, to call her Bonnie.

"Is that your name in English?" I ask.

"It's what my mother-in-law called me," Asnakech says.

"What would you rather be called?" I ask.

"Asnakech," she says, then repeats it phonetically: "As-NAK-ech."

She is the only female miller in Ethiopia, and has been fixated on establishing Amaro as its own specific coffee region in Ethiopia. She wants to bring Amaro to the world—and then to bring the riches of the world back to Amaro. To follow Asnakech anywhere is to learn what is possible from the Ethiopian land. She picks up pieces of plants and crouches constantly atop the surrounding soil. Avocados, sugarcane, castor beans, bananas, enset, peppers, and coffee run through her fingers and fill her stories.

The Amaro tribe is said to have come from the Christian north, in Gonder, and traveled south via Arba Minch, crossing the mountains eastward to present-day Amaro. Amara, as they called it first, translated to "it is beautiful."

The Amaros settled here because of the thick forests and options for agriculture. Today, slightly less than two hundred thousand people live in this valley. If you ask Asnakech, they are all her cousins, aunts, and uncles. She was born and raised here, and has come back for the coffee.

"When I was young," she tells me, "we had coffee the size of tomatoes. The mountains were that full of fruit—or that is what they said. They would find cherries and peel them like an orange. Imagine, coffee the size of tomatoes." Her eyes widen as if trying to become the size of tomatoes themselves: "Imagine."

Opposite: **Fertile land in Amaro.**
Right: **Woizero Asnakech Thomas.**

COFFEE PEACE

Buna Kala created and maintained peace throughout Amaro's past. Similar to Buna Kele in Harar, sun-dried coffee beans of a nearly homogenous size were gathered and bit off at the tip. Next they were boiled in butter and cooked so that the butter infused the coffee cherry—roasting it from the inside. The beans were then strained from the mix and added to a pot of hot milk with sugar and honey. The custom was to pass around a *moko* (wooden spoon) of Buna Kala. Everyone in a dispute would drink from the same spoon and thus resolve their differences.

Left: Woizero Wogayhu pulverizes coffee grounds in a homemade mortar and pestle.
Opposite: Woizero Asnakech Thomas outside her new mill in Derbe Menana.

TWO IN A BOX

Asnakech was twelve when she was kidnapped and taken from her family in Kele, the central town at the base of the Amaro Mountains. She tells me this matter-of-factly one night over coffee following dinner. "You know," she says, "it happens, because my family was one of the ones who would not give me away."

She was forced to marry, and had two children by the time she was fourteen. She ran away and was caught, twice. She was blindfolded and taken to new homes. The third time she tried to escape, she was successful. She left Amaro then rather than risk being caught again.

In the years that followed, Asnakech lived in Addis, moved to Italy, came back to Addis, started a cheese company, baked wedding cakes, moved to England, married a man from England, had more children, started more than a half-dozen agricultural businesses, and eventually came home to Amaro.

"I have done many things," she says. "But the one thing I really want to do is build a hospital in Kele."

She goes on to tell me about the women in Kele, who, if their labor is progressing poorly, have to travel 150 kilometers for a hospital. "These women?" Asnakech says. "They usually come home two in a box."

"The mother and the baby?" I ask.

"Together in one box," Asnakech says.

Her sister lost her life and child this way. The last Asnakech's family saw of her sister was a wooden box containing the woman's stillborn child and her birthing-ravaged body. "And if not that," Asnakech says, "she could have had a fistula. And then what would have happened to her in Kele, with no hospital?"

An obstetric fistula is a complication during birth that results in death of the mother's tissue and a corresponding hole through which urine and/or feces leak. An estimated one hundred fifty thousand women in Ethiopia are living with fistulas, and are usually abandoned by their husbands and cast aside to live with the animals outside their family homes.

"I am lucky," Asnakech says. "But my sisters have not been. I have lost two this way. The women in Kele are not always lucky."

Asnakech scoots her chair to follow the disappearing midday shade. "Coffee can change this," she says.

All around her are innovations in coffee picking, processing, and cultivation. She will stay at her mountain mill for another week after we leave. She will work with farmers to try to find new coffees, and then protect those coffees as best she can. "A little more money—why not? This is our green gold," she says. "Today, it is already better if we take care of it."

She reaches into her pocket and pulls out a sun-dried cherry. She bites into it, chews, and spits it out. "It is not ready yet," she says. "Soon it will be the best you have ever tasted." She settles in to wait.

SPINNING COFFEE TALES & COTTON

Woizero Fetlework brings her spinning tools to the afternoon coffee. She has graying hair plaited into braids that somehow both hide and accentuate her hair's changing color, so that you have to catch the light just right to see any mid-braid whitening.

Her name means "spinner of gold," so given because her mother gave birth to her after a whole day spinning by herself. Woizero Fetlework, too, became a spinner and has supported her family by making and selling clothing. Coffee helps her measure her days.

"In one day," she tells me, "ten to twenty women can make a *gabi*." She is referring to the thick white cotton cloth used for clothing and as a blanket throughout Ethiopia. "We spin, brew coffee, and when the coffee is done, the gabi is done," she says.

When I ask her how coffee came to Amaro, Woizero Fetlework grows quiet and pulls her cotton thread tight several times on the spindle before answering.

"This king now," she says, referring to the king of the Amaro, "is fourteen generations. Twelve generations before that were the ones before. The first kings? I don't know. Another fourteen generations." The cotton strand between her hands snaps, and she expertly tethers it back to itself. "A long time," she concludes.

"Forty generations," I say.

"A long time," she says again.

Right: Woizero Fetlework and Woizero Wogayhu spin cotton in Amaro Kele.
Opposite left: Coffee from awol, the first round.
Opposite right: Abo Awajo in Amaro Kele.

RESOLUTION IN A BEAN

Abo Awajo joins Woizero Fetlework, Asnakech, and me in the garden for coffee. He tells me that coffee keeps peace even today. "If I have a long-standing conflict with someone," he says, "and an elder comes to my home to mediate when coffee is roasting or brewing, I will accept his mediation without any question."

"Are there exceptions?" I ask.

"Never. Coffee changes everything. If there is a bitter shouting match, all of it quiets when the coffee ceremony starts. It is the practice."

Abo Awajo takes a sip of coffee and leans back into his chair to savor it. His eyes narrow at me before he speaks again.

"Did you know that even if someone dies in the middle of having coffee, that we will wait until we finish the coffee before we tend to the dead?"

I look at Woizero Fetlework to see if he is telling the truth. She nods.

"Despite the depth of people's grief," Abo says, "this is what we do."

Earlier, the women placed fresh, thick enset leaves under Abo's feet as a symbol of respect; the tips of the leaves pointed outward, in the direction from which he came. Now he shuffles his feet on the glossy surface.

"When a suitor's family comes to my home to ask for my daughter's hand in marriage, if they are lucky, they time it when the household is roasting or brewing coffee. If this happens, I have no choice but to grant his request," he says.

I ask Abo Awajo how many daughters he's married off because of a suitor's luck with timing.

"We drink coffee all of the time," he says. "And I have many daughters."

The women around him laugh. "No," he says, "I only have to give them away if they come during awol, first cup."

In Amaro, one's timing with a coffee ceremony can dictate fate. If an unexpected visitor arrives during awol, it is good luck; but second-cup arrivals are treated with suspicion. "They are usually gossipmongers," Abo Awajo says. "It is the worst luck to come then."

"And the third cup, baraka?" I ask. "What does arrival then suggest?"

"Peace," Abo says.

Right: Some 159 girls and 142 boys attend school at Doorbadi. They line up together every morning to raise the Ethiopian flag. The school is only ten years old. Previously, the children had to walk more than seven miles into Amaro proper for classes. Today, in English class, they are on Lesson Twenty: "Is she short, fat, happy, sick, young?" asks the textbook caption beside a picture of a girl. I think she looks to be all of them. A seven-year-old tells me the girl is clearly short; the pupil says this in Kurate, the language of the region. Her teacher, in English, tells her that she is correct.

Opposite left: Coffee prepared from the leaves is an orange butterscotch color when it leaves the jebena. Although you can see through the stream, when the coffee pools in your cup it is thick and rich. Garlic, tennadum, and ginger all infuse the brew. Its strength can be felt just from the smell.

Opposite right: Here (and elsewhere in Ethiopia), teff is processed by animal power. This man has spent the past hour covering a circular arena with a layer of wet manure before bringing in his grain. The manure will harden and provide an easy surface off which to gather the individual grains.

AMARO HIGHLANDS

Yero Walla is the tallest mountain in the Amaro Range. Today, we circumnavigate it to get to the other side. It's been raining in the mountains, and the earthen roads are unstable and slippery. Travel timing is critical, and we wait for the day's heat to dry the road's top layer before starting. It is a two-day walk for farmers to bring their coffee cherries down to Kele. A year ago, Asnakech Thomas built a mill on the eastern side of the Amaro Range, and now farmers have the option to trade the cherry directly in the high hills. Even to drive this distance, thirty-five kilometers, is a day's effort. Here, the word "road" guarantees only that you'll find a relatively flat span just wide enough for six people to walk abreast.

We creep lazily upward, leaving the coffee land and entering the drier plateaus. We round a two-thousand-meter pass and descend back into opulent green. Foraging goats (absent this day) have evenly "mowed" the grass, creating a manicured feeling within this wild land. Acacia trees grow up at an angle that maintains their perfect horizontal canopies. We pass the temporary wooden corrals of pastoral Guji families, the fenced spaces empty for now. We are the only ones on the road today. No other car has passed for a week. We know we are in the Derbe Menana region by the dried coffee in the road. It fills space usually unoccupied, but today we drive over the coffee and crack the cherries in the potholes. In Ethiopia's coffee regions, roads double as drying space anywhere traffic is sparse.

UNTOUCHABLE EVERYDAY

Ethiopia has a longstanding practice of caste discrimination that places people who work with metal, leather, and earth at a lower level of economic, social, and human valuation than the country's other craftspeople. Jebenas—Ethiopia's ubiquitous coffee pots—are handmade by this caste. In larger cities, the lines of differentiation have begun to blur, but here in the high mountains, to visit the people who make the jebenas, we have to go to the dwelling region of the "untouchables."

The type of land people are allowed to occupy often conveys social status in Ethiopia. Here in Derbe Menana, the best land is the higher hills; the land immediately surrounding the steep riverbeds, given to erosion and harder to cultivate, is left for the untouchables.

Across the river and set in deep morning shade, the wood is already burning hot for today's jebena firing. Each jebena is made from clay excavated just above the river, and then hand-molded into a rounded shape with a tight neck to trap the heat. The surface is first smoothed with a river stone, then leather, then cloth. To keep them from collapsing, the lids and pots dry on an elevated bed of dried coffee cherries. Today—Wednesday—is firing day. By nightfall, there will be more than sixty new jebenas ready to leave the hillside and make their way to the homes of the higher castes, homes where the artisans themselves are not allowed to enter.

Here at Asnakech Thomas' new mill, 50 percent of her workforce is determined by a lottery every week. She rotates her temporary workers via this system. For her, the standard is if they are "believers." If they are Christian enough, work is theirs, untouchable or not.

Right: **Drying ceramic pot lids in Derbe Menana.**
Opposite: **Sun-dried coffee cherries in Derbe Menana.**

COFFEE STORY: ETHIOPIA

THE MESSA OF MARSHA

Marsha Aday and his wife, Gete Tebo, live in a house without a door on the flanks of Mount Yero Wallo. It is the only home here without a door, but Marsha Aday says this lack does not matter. The threshold opens on a flat field with views of anyone who approaches. "No one or no thing," he says, "dares attack me."

He tells me he knew I was coming an hour before I got here. By the time I arrived, his family had set up a seating area outside. I'm given the largest chair; it has a seat of animal hide, its legs thick and sturdy with lowland wood. Marsha Aday sits across from me on a smaller chair, perched on an incline so that his line of sight is higher than mine. We meet in the middle.

Marsha Aday is forty and leader of the Messa tribe in the Marsha region. He was an only child, and his father is still the keeper of the Messa tribal history.

"Coffee did not come here from people," he tells me, "but through nature." Wef Zerash is the name for natural seed dispersal through the birds and animals that moved coffee into the region. Marsha Aday's tribe knew of the cherries, but did not use them.

"Muslims would come from Kereda, and bought coffee beans by the capful and carried them away on their camels," he says, "but we did not use the coffee. We thought the seeds would burn us." He picks up a red cherry as if to make me wonder if this might still be possible.

"Over time, the Guji came to buy our coffee as well. Eventually, the Messa started to use the beans themselves. Never the leaves, though," he says, shaking his head emphatically. "Drinking the leaves is bad form."

Marsha Aday and I both use our hands when we talk. We constantly interrupt the narrow space of dirt between us with the blur of our variously gesticulating hands. We speak through a translator, who stands out of the way. He keeps his hands at his sides. Soon, we barely need him.

Marsha Aday, Gete Tebo, and their children in Marsha.

AN ACCIDENTAL RAIN DANCE

When I arrive, Marsha Aday looks like any other Messa man. The afternoon light grows long and burns away our shade, next to his house. Clouds gather in the far corner of the western sky. "It will rain soon," Marsha Aday says. "Before it does, I will show you what makes the Messa different."

He goes into his hut with his wife and comes outside adorned. He tells me his headdress is called a Kalacha; meanwhile, his cape is made of lion mane and trimmed in silver. His necklace, Joshe, means "big." His royal regalia is seven generations old, and will be passed on to his eldest son for the eighth generation. Marsha Aday's seven children surround him now. They are excited, because he usually saves his costume for special occasions. An ox is customarily slaughtered for ceremony, and coffee is drunk. Marsha Aday tells me I am the reason for his dressing up today. "And now," he says, "you must at least stay for coffee." He smiles and adds, "It is too late in the day for an ox."

When Marsha Aday performs his traditional tribal celebration dance, he crouches low and leaps high, shaking a shield in one hand to accentuate his baritone chanting. His knees lift up inside his lion cape, and his voice carries through the thickening air. The silver atop his shoulders dances on its attachment points, its jingling accompanying his voice. His children watch, the younger ones jumping up and down as they try to imitate their father. The clouds are amassing now, the light diffused as it reflects off the royal crown. My translator is worried about the weather, as is Marsha Aday's cousin, who brought us here. But I am not yet ready to leave, and Marsha Aday seems to know this when he asks me inside.

We all pack into the round home together. Gete has been readying a coffee ceremony. The air is damp and fragrant with myrrh so that it smells sweet and musty. Marsha Aday sits facing the front threshold. His youngest children, three years and eighteen months, each clutch one of his legs. He picks up the littlest one. "This one," he says, giving his son a squeeze on his belly until the baby squeals with laughter, "drinks coffee as if he were suckling at the breast."

Like the Amaro, the Messa believe that luck is granted to anyone who arrives during the first cup of coffee. "Even a person who comes with the intention of killing another and arrives during abol will set his plans aside," Marsha Aday says.

Coffee is plentiful here, so much so that Marsha Aday tells me there is coffee he has seen on trees but never seen picked. There are no roads or trails to these trees, and hence no way for the cherries to leave the trees. "If you come back," he tells me, "I will take you there. This coffee—it is our gold. It puts our entire country on the world map."

AN UNFINISHED CUP

The rain starts in the distance. The thunder booms and claps, and Marsha Aday can see the storm coming. I keep my back to the open door. I want one more story. Gete is starting up the fire and roasting coffee beans. I wonder how many layers of coffee scent infuse this home.

Marsha Aday watches me inhale deeply. "The coffee will be ready soon," he tells me.

In the meantime, he indulges me by using his hands to pantomime a story of how his tribe used to drink coffee from flutes made of buffalo horns. He explains that the custom survived even until his childhood, when important individuals would still receive their coffee in the flutes, the others in ceramic cups. He reaches to pick up a modern cup to show me when a thunderclap shakes all ten tiny cups on the tray. The beans on the pan pop in the background. Soon it will be time to grind them with the stone mortar and pestle.

Concerned onlookers fill the threshold. The light from outside disappears. "It will start," they all say to me. "Soon. You must go." They will not move until I get up. And they are right.

The big, wet African raindrops feel luxurious coming from the sky. They catch me between my eyes and on the tip of my nose. I run for the mill. Within minutes of rain, everything is slick and wet. I am chilled for the first time since I arrived in Ethiopia. New rivers form instantly before me, running milky brown with froth down the hillside. I follow them to my temporary home.

Thirty minutes after leaving Marsha Aday, I huddle with the evening workers at the mill. A ceiling of sisal coffee sacks and plastic tarps covers us. As the rain grows stronger, we gather closer. The noise on our makeshift roof is too loud for talking. The sound is enough to listen to anyway.

I don't yet know it, but the following day we will barely be able to leave. The mud will settle just under the ground's surface, and our tires will hardly grip the road—and when they do, they will send us in the wrong direction, slipping down the hillside. It will take twenty people and three tries to pull us from the ditch. While we work to free the truck, I will have to keep myself from disappearing back into the forest. It might not be so bad to stay in Derbe Menana, I will find myself thinking. I could go back to visit Marsha Aday. We would finally be able to have our coffee.

Inside Marsha Aday and Gete Tebo's home.

AFTERWORD

Halfway through my 2009 trip to Ethiopia, I sat down with a series of academics who had devoted the greater part of their lives—a collective two hundred years—to studying the country. The professor Richard Pankhurst, academic Rita Pankhurst, Addis Ababa museum curator Amhed Zekaria, researcher Amsaya Anteneh, and the professor Gezahegn Berecha Yadessa were just some of the erudite experts who shared their knowledge of Ethiopian culture. To each, I put this question: "That you know of, has there been significant research on the cultural resonance of coffee in Ethiopia?" All answered in the negative. Rita Pankhurst had done the most extensive research, for a paper she published in 1997, though she primarily focused on the origins of the coffee ceremony. I am indebted to her exhaustive work.

Each time I learned of the limited scope of the prior cultural research, I was in equal parts overwhelmed, excited, and awed. The reason for these limits had to do with simple economics—any money given to studying coffee in Ethiopia has always been to increase the plant's disease resistance and yield. The cultural meaning of coffee—the "softer" side of its science—was passed over in light of the need for practicality. I see *Coffee Story: Ethiopia* as part of a larger dialogue on Ethiopia's coffee heritage. My hope is that this book is the start of many more similar collections of tales, be they shared orally or in print volumes to follow.

I welcome new stories. I hope we all get to hear them soon.

Opposite: **Menelik Alemu and Majka Burhardt, Lake Tana.**
Right: **Mohammed Abdo Aidir in Hirna.**

ACKNOWLEDGEMENTS

This book is only possible because of the willingness and generosity of my Ethiopian friends. Thank you for allowing me into your homes, lives, and stories: Ubah Ali Abdullahi, Sheik Abdullah Abrit, Marsha Aday, Mohammed Abdo Aidir, Menelik Alemu, Abo Awajo, Haji Abdul Basitt, Sha'le Bokal, Woizero Fetlework, Muhammed Gunde, Abera Kebede, Gebremedhim Kidame, Aba Gebre Mechan, Abshire Seman Nuri, Guled Osman Omar, Amir Redwan, Silvio Rizzotti, Fatuma Siti, Abrar Sualeh, Gete Tebo, Tamagn Tedesse, German Wendafrash, Girma Wendafrash, Woizero Wogayhu, Ato Yumatoma, and many others.

I offer up a profound thank-you to Travis Horn for his unmatched enthusiasm while shooting the photography for this book. This book lives and breathes because of his fine work.

I'd like to thank Teddy Berhanu for his insights, humor, and constant additions to stories and perspectives; Semeon Abay for his hard work and light heart; and Yemi Tessema for her translation skills and continued support of the project.

I'm grateful to the following people for their additions and perspectives: Abdul Ahmed, Irene Angelico, Amsaya Anteneh, Raf Arefs, Abdullah Bagersh, Gassan Bagersh, Omar Bagersh, Yaregal Fenthum, Rob Gordon, Kit Kuntze, Elizabeth O'Neill, Richard Pankhurst, Rita Pankhurst, Mark Pendergrast, Ric Rhinehardt, Donald Schoenholt, Asnakech Thomas, Gezahegn Berecha Yadessa, Habtamu Yaregal, and Amhed Zekaria.

Matt Samet, my editor and friend, is a steady source of encouragement and perspective. Designer Margery Cantor took a leap into this project and gave it beauty and wisdom.

Opposite: **Pelican above Lake Tana.**
Above: **Ato Sha'le Bokal receiving his personal copy of *Coffee Story: Ethiopia*.**

I owe a deep debt of gratitude to everyone who supported the first edition of this book, and who demanded a second. I could never have imagined the response and interest—from the Philippines to British Columbia, from Tokyo to Flagstaff, Arizona, from coffee shops to the coffee tables of people passionate about understanding our world. Thank you, all, for opening these pages, and for opening your heart and mind to Ethiopia. Thank you especially to Mary Anna Novek, Susanne Conrad, and Sapna Dayal for holding space with me for this edition to be possible.

I would also like to acknowledge and thank the following people for their help with the first edition, without which this second edition would not have been possible: Joseph Brodsky, Steven Holt, and Zak Phillips. I'd also like to extend deep gratitude to Herb Brodsky, who, a long time ago at a coffee shop in Boulder, Colorado, sold me on caring about coffee.

And lastly, thanks to my family and friends, who constantly support and encourage me. Thank you especially to Peter, for letting me, and Ethiopia, into your life in every way possible. And thank you to my children, Kaz and Irenna, for sharing your first year with the creation of this second edition.

GLOSSARY

Abadir: Often used as the name for the coffee tree in Ethiopia, named after Sheik Abadir. Sheik Abadir was the first emir of Harar, in the thirteenth century, though many place Sheik Abadir, namesake of the coffee tree, in the ninth century.

Abol: Used to describe the first round/first cup of coffee; derived from the Arabic *awwal*, meaning "first, old, preceding." See also *awol*.

Ashara: An Oromo name for a drink made from coffee husks, often consumed in the eastern highlands.

Ato: Used as a term of respect before men's first names.

Awol: Used to describe the first round/first cup of coffee; derived from the Arabic *awwal*, meaning "first, old, preceding." See also *abol*.

Awwal: Arabic word for "first, old, preceding." See also *abol* and *awol*.

Baraka: Arabic for "blessing"; used to describe the third round/third cup of coffee.

Berbere: A mixture of ground hot red peppers and other spices used throughout Ethiopia as a key ingredient in meal preparation. See also *burburri*.

Bun: A variation of *buna*.

Buna: The most commonly used name for coffee in Ethiopia. See also *bun*, *bunn*, and *bunni*.

Buna Sirri: A Harari ritual meal involving a thick barley pancake topped with dried coffee cherries in butter.

Bunn: A variation of *buna*.

Bunni: A variation of *buna*.

Burburri: A mixture of ground hot red peppers and other spices used throughout Ethiopia as a key ingredient in meal preparation. See also *berbere*.

Chat: A leafy plant used as an amphetamine-like stimulant, legally harvested and sold in Ethiopia. See also *khat* and *qat*.

Chemo: The name for the coffee tea brewed from coffee leaves in Kaffa.

Enjera: A fermented pancake bread made of teff (a high-protein grain) that's cooked on a clay griddle over an open fire.

Enset: Also called false banana, enset is an Ethiopian staple and one of its most effective measures against hunger—one root-bundle can provide up to forty kilograms of food.

Farange: Used to refer to foreigners throughout Ethiopia.

Fota: A headscarf worn by women that still leaves the face exposed.

Gabi: A woven all-purpose cotton garment used as a blanket, dress, shawl, or rug.

Hasher: A brew made from coffee husks consumed in Harar.

Hoja: The Harari word for the tea made from coffee husks; usually brewed with milk.

Hulatena: Used to describe the second round/second cup of coffee. See also *tala*, *thani*, *tola*, and *tona*.

Jebena: An earthenware pot with a round belly and narrow neck used to make coffee.

Kaf: Arabic for "enough."

Kaffa: A region in southwestern Ethiopia; previously its own kingdom.

Kelo: A practice wherein coffee beans are roasted in butter until they reach their height of potency, and then tucked between cheeks and gums to allow a constant flow of caffeine.

Khat: A leafy plant used as an amphetamine-like stimulant legally harvested and sold in Ethiopia. See also *chat* and *qat*.

Kuti: The name for tea made from coffee leaves in Harar; also called Kuti Kela.

Meg: A two-piece grinder made of volcanic stone used to pulverize corn and coffee.

Moko: A wooden spoon used for Buna Kala in the Amaro Mountains.

Netala: A cotton shawl woven in Ethiopia and worn by women.

Qahwa: An Arabic word used for wine made from coffee.

Qat: A leafy plant used as an amphetamine-like stimulant legally harvested and sold in Ethiopia. See also *chat* and *khat*.

Rekebot: The tray used in the coffee ceremony.

Shagna: The fatty meat from the large cervicothoracic hump on Ethiopian cows.

Sirri: A barley pancake eaten in Harar.

Tala: Used to describe the second round/second cup of coffee. See also *hulatena*, *thani*, *tola*, and *tona*.

Tankwa: The papyrus boats found on Lake Tana.

Teff: A high-protein grain used throughout Ethiopia.

Tennadum: Rue, often placed in cups of coffee throughout Ethiopia.

Thani: Arabic for "second"; used to describe the second round/second cup of coffee. See also *hulatena*, *tala*, *tola*, and *tona*.

Tola: Used to describe the second round/second cup of coffee. See also *hulatena*, *tala*, *thani*, and *tona*.

Tona: Used to describe the second round/second cup of coffee. See also *hulatena*, *tala*, *thani*, and *tola*.

Wahber: The name for an "empty" coffee bean used in the Buna Sirri ceremony in Harar.

Woizero/Woizerit: Used as a term of respect before women's first names—Woizero if the woman is married, Woizerit if she is unmarried.

Sunrise, Addis Ababa.

REFERENCES

Angelico, Irene (dir.). *Black Coffee: The Irresistible Bean* (DVD). Delphis Films, 2005.

de Waal, Alex. *Evil Days: 30 Years of War and Famine in Ethiopia.* Human Rights Watch, 1997.

Gilbert, Elizabeth. *Tribes of the Great Rift Valley.* New York: Abrams, 2007.

Gill, Peter. *Famine and Foreigners: Ethiopia Since Live Aid.* London: Oxford, 2010.

Gordon, Robert. *Picturing Bushman: The Denver African Expedition of 1925.* Ohio: Ohio University Press, 1997.

Haile, Rebecca G. *Held At a Distance: A Rediscovery of Ethiopia.* Chicago: Academy Chicago, 2007.

Henze, Paul. *Ethiopia in Mengistu's Final Years,* vols 1 and 2. Addis Ababa: Shama Books, 2007.

Kapuscinski, Richard. *The Emperor: Downfall of an Autocrat.* New York: Vintage International, 1983.

Lorenzetti, Linda Rice. *The Birth of Coffee.* New York: Clarkston Potter, 2000.

Marsden, Philip. *The Chains of Heaven: An Ethiopian Romance.* London: Harper Perennial, 2005.

Pankhurst, Rita. "The Coffee Ceremony and the History of Coffee Consumption in Ethiopia," *Ethiopia in Broader Perspective, Papers of the XIIIth International Conference of Ethiopian Studies,* Volume II. 516-539. Kyoto, 1997.

Pendergrast, Mark. *Uncommon Grounds.* New York: Basic Books, 1999.

Reader, John. *Africa: The Biography of the Continent.* London: Hamish Hamilton Ltd, 1997.

Stiglitz, Joseph. *Globalization and its Discontents.* New York: Penguin Books, 2002.

Zewde, *Bahru. Pioneers of Change in Ethiopia: Reformist Intellectuals of the Early Twentieth Century.* Ohio: Ohio University Press, 2002.

Roasted, ground coffee for sale in Harar.

ABOUT THE AUTHOR, PHOTOGRAPHER, & ARTIST

Coffee Story: Ethiopia is the second book authored by **Majka Burhardt,** who in 2008 published *Vertical Ethiopia: Climbing Toward Possibility in the Horn of Africa* (Shama Books). Ms. Burhardt is also producer and director of the film *Namuli* (2016) and executive producer of *Waypoint Namibia* (2010). Burhardt is the founder and executive director of Legado, where she works to protect the world's most threatened mountain ecosystems by empowering the people who call them home. Legado originated during a pioneering climbing and conservation research expedition to Mozambique. Ms. Burhardt holds an MFA in creative writing from the Warren Wilson Program for Writers, and received her BA in anthropology from Princeton University. She lives in New Hampshire with her husband, Peter, and twins, Kaz and Irenna. *Majkaburhardt.com*

Travis Horn has cultivated a photography career born from a pursuit of "foreign familiarity," realizing documentary editorials in the Caribbean, Central and South America, Europe, Asia, and Africa. His work has been showcased by *National Geographic Adventure, Gourmand,* and Hyatt International Hotels, with recent exhibitions in Beijing, Port au Prince, and Miami. Horn's involvement with the specialty-coffee industry has spanned multiple creative endeavors in coffee-origin countries including Panama, Costa Rica, Colombia, and Ethiopia. In 2014, Horn travelled to Beijing to exhibit portraits from *Coffee Story: Ethiopia* and to accept the "Best Photography in a Food and Beverage category, Africa" award from *Gourmand.*

Molly Holmberg Brown is a visual artist, mapmaker, and geographer. She discovered cartography at Middlebury College and went on to receive a PhD in human geography from the University of Colorado Boulder. She received a Watson Fellowship and a National Science Foundation Fellowship to explore the value of mapmaking for communities and individuals. Brown has worked in environmental and art education for organizations, universities, and schools across the country. Her current projects involve mapmaking with children, conveying climate change through landscape painting, and custom maps for place-based organizations. *Mollymaps.com*